Praise from ~~Rea~~

THE WISDOM OF GRIEF:

" The feeling of reading this is one of a healing embrace."

"A transformative account of faith and redemption."

"With tears at the prologue and I read on continuously, completely absorbed. Written with complete intimacy and candor with the deepest of integrity."

"AMAZING! I couldn't stop. So raw and honest. The structure is perfect."

"THANK YOU for the gift of this book, which has completely shifted my thinking about my own grief. I no longer see it as misery but as a journey of courage."

"I read it straight through, with a lot of choking up. What an accomplishment, especially the format, which puts the distilling of personal experience at the service of others."

"Brave and beautiful."

THE WISDOM OF GRIEF:

Mining the Treasure Inherent in Great Loss

Leslie Palumbo, LCSW

Publishers Cataloging-in-Publication
(Provided by Quality Books, Inc.)

Palumbo, Leslie.

The wisdom of grief: mining the treasure inherent in great loss / Leslie Palumbo, LCSW. – First Edition.

pages cm

Includes bibliographic references.

ISBN 978-0-9862781-0-5

1. Bereavement   2. Loss (Psychology)   3. Palumbo, Leslie.   I. Title

BF575.G7P35 2015   155.9'37

QB115-600058

Printed in The United States of America

1   3 5 7 9 10 8 6 4 2

Book Design by Miranda Borden
Huntdesign1@gmail.com

For J & Nicholas

No man who is surrounded by love is ever marooned.
~Robert Louis Stevenson

For Julia, Miranda & Dad

Peace is every step. ~Thich Nhat Hahn

CONTENTS

When the doors of perception are cleansed,
man will see things as they truly are, infinite.

~William Blake

INTRODUCTION

There is nobody on the planet, neither those whom we see as the oppressed nor those whom we see as the oppressor, who doesn't have what it takes to wake up.
~ *Pema Chodron*

Life is a journey, and at some point on this journey, if we live long enough, we will experience great loss. Something we never thought was possible suddenly happens. We had heard about tragedy happening around us, read about awful misfortune and catastrophe in the news, but it felt far removed from our own experience. *That is terrible- I feel so lucky that it is not happening to me,* we had always thought. But suddenly it is happening to us. We are involved in a terrible accident. We or someone we love gets terminal cancer, or perishes. Our spouse walks out on us. Our child dies. Someone we love is murdered. A family member commits suicide.

In these moments, it is as if the sky opens up and sucks up what we knew of life, leaving only space and the accompanying suffering. For a while we bang our heads against the wall trying to fit this event into our current understanding of the world. But try as we might, the puzzle piece does not seem to fit into the larger picture. We are forced to change our vision of the world. We are pressured open. We are invited to expand.

Is there a way to make this easier on ourselves?

In our increasingly hurried culture, we don't allow much room for grief. We think that we have to be quick about it; to get over it as rapidly as possible. We are encouraged not to dwell in difficult places. Society imposes time limits and expectations for how long to grieve, and these time limits have

{ 1 }

grown exponentially shorter in recent years. A hundred years ago, the acceptable time to mourn a spouse was between two and three years. Now we suggest anywhere from several weeks to 6 months. If we do not move beyond a loss in the timeframe set about by professionals, it is considered abnormal. The recently released DSM-5, or Diagnostic and Statistical Manual of Mental Disorders, has created a new diagnosis, called Persistent Complex Bereavement Related Disorder, which involves remaining grief symptoms occurring at least one year after the death of a loved one.

The question is, what do we miss when we rush ourselves through such a sacred experience?

Grief is a universal experience. It is not a pathological state, though it often feels like it is. It is a normal, adaptive process which helps us evolve as individuals and as a species. Character is formed in the spaces left behind by great loss. One example of this is the development of emotional resilience, an important characteristic which helps us through the loss that is a natural part of all life. Another is the increase in emotional intelligence that occurs as we experience new heights of empathy, endurance, mercy, and so many more of our finest human qualities.

It is said that without inner peace, there will always be turbulence around us, and that increased world harmony is only possible through increased sentimental insight. Would we deprive ourselves of this opportunity to make ourselves, and the world, into a more openhearted, magnanimous place?

Grief is a stopping point, a sacred moment. It is an opportunity to feel the most vital parts of what it means to be human, not the least of which is life's fragility. The reality is that when someone is mourning, instead of offering our sympathy, we should be offering our deep reverence for the formidable path they are walking, as well as our compassion and respect.

Mourning allows us to slow down, or stop traveling at the same velocity as the rest of the world for a time. We begin to notice different things. We may stop noticing some very unpleasant aspects of life; traffic, noise pollution, or other disturbances, and find other aspects, often more subtle and lasting; kindness, connection, and the quiet vibration of tears. Grief opens us up to our best human qualities: the strength of the human spirit, the value of compassion, and the grace that comes with a gentle ceaseless patience in the face of life's limits. But if we rush through it, we will miss the treasure inherent in any great loss.

When sudden misfortune occurs, everything in our being tells us to run from the pain. However, it is actually an especially good time to pay attention and stay with it. There is gold to be mined from our deepest suffering. The profoundest insights are often found when sudden space enters our experience. Accessing the precious moments on the journey helps us not to become stuck at any one point, and enables us to move fluidly into our future, embracing the full gifts that life has to offer us all along the way.

Grief connects us to the present moment. Life takes on a timeless quality. The beauty of this is that what we cherish most- love, aliveness, creativity, play- arise only in moments of presence and clarity. So when we experience great loss, we have a greater access to what is sacred and precious in life.

The problem can be that we are unable to see this through the fog of suffering. When we are suffering, we often do not have the space to see events from a larger perspective. We mistake our suffering for who we are. This is why we must grant ourselves time and practices which allow us to stay with the pain and ride it through its natural course. Some kind of contemplative practice helps us to separate actual pain from the suffering we create in an effort to protect ourselves from that pain. There are some transcendent things that happen in the midst of grief, but if we get too attached to the story of suffering that grief carries with it, we cannot feel these other aspects.

Often, we are afraid to talk about the positive aspects of grief and great loss because we think it will somehow dishonor the severity and immensity of what has happened. Because it feels forced upon us, because we never asked for it, we think we have to resist it. Part of us may believe that if we feel good in the midst of mourning, it will reflect poorly on the person we have lost- as if their life has less value for our having grown from the loss of it.

* * *

This book is partly the story of what happened to me the day the sky of my world opened up and I fell through. The event that precipitated this was by far the worst thing that had ever occurred in my life. It was definitely beyond my imagination or my worst fears. And yet it happened. One radiant Indian summer morning, almost too perfect for the eyes, my mother walked out of her house to the end of her dock on the quiet shore of a Virginia river and shot herself in the head with a small .22 caliber gun.

The anguish and confusion this brought to our family was unlike anything I had known was possible. How had this happened? It was not like she had been on the verge of suicide all of her life. Or had she? I was a psychotherapist. I had years of training in the dysfunctions of the mind. How could I have missed the signs? Saving people had been my mission in life. How could I not have saved my own mother? My mind was crowded with a multitude of questions but no answers. The only thing I knew for certain was that I was no longer certain about anything at all.

My mother's suicide was the most shocking, horrifying thing that I could have ever envisioned. I think of myself as an intuitive and empathetic person. I can also be an anxious person, one who in a state of worry runs all possible dramas and tragedies through my mind as a way of trying to prepare myself for whatever life might throw at me. So in this regard, I thought I had covered every possible angle of painful possibilities in this life. As a professional, I thought I was sensitive enough to recognize, anticipate, or at least suspect something of this magnitude in my own family. However, I was completely unprepared for this event. The violence, suddenness, and aberration of it upset the natural order of life in every way.

I knew that my mother was in a depressive breakdown. I had been increasingly concerned about how to help her. And yet in all of my worry, the realistic possibility of her suicide had simply never occurred to me at all. It is just not something she would have done. It was not in her character in any way. She had always been petrified of death.

As a psychotherapist, I became fascinated by the process of my grief. For years I had worked with clients in mourning- as individuals, in small groups, workshops, and in meditation groups. Now here I was witnessing this person who was disintegrating- she would find herself driving the wrong way toward a destination; she was unable to read; she forgot what she was saying in the middle of a sentence; she often had to simply retreat into her bed- and that person was me.

When my mother committed suicide, I had been meditating for several years, engaged in the study and practice of present moment awareness as a path to feeling life more richly and to dealing with the strong emotional suffering from the past that kept reappearing in my present. Ironically, the unlikely experience of my mother's abrupt, violent death allowed me to fall off a precipice of fear into an intense state of awareness in which I felt a peace, joy and love so profound that any words I could use to describe it would be as pitiful as the size of the smallest amoeba in comparison to a great blue whale. This deep sense of peace coexisted with the pain and suffering I was undergoing, and on a universal level I found this paradox fascinating. Alongside this, and as the intense period of awake passed, I felt a deep yearning to make some kind of sense out of the senseless event of my mother's suicide. I wanted to understand how this fit into the larger enigma that is life. It did not seem right for her to have died this way and have nothing but pain come out of it.

I became convinced that the way to mine the gems in the loss lay in taking a greater perspective- coming to an understanding that did not narrow the experience but rather stretched it so that it could be seen from all angles. For me the way to this open view lay in connecting with something greater than my intellect. Through all of the grieving, raging, puzzling about my mother, and self examination, I felt my hands, I felt my feet, I remembered that I was larger than my mind and more than my sometimes overwhelming emotions. I practiced making contact with a greater force than my often small-minded, suffering self. I have included the mindfulness practices which I found helpful during the various phases of my mourning. The contemplations arose organically out of the experience.

As I mourned, I noticed that, coinciding with the various common stages on the journey of grieving, there are many openings, or cracks through which we can see life in a new way. Some passageways we recognize and others are more difficult to see, but all of these apertures offer opportunities to expand into a greater version of ourselves as human beings. They contain the possibility for us to access and strengthen all of the best of our human qualities: empathy, kindness, love, patience, strength, perspective, joy, wisdom, and compassion.

Each chapter of the book begins with The Story: a phase of my personal grieving, followed by A Greater Perspective, which offers professional and spiritual perspective on the particular aspect of mourning described in the chapter, as well as a specific Gift of Grief revealed. The end of each chapter is an Antidote to Grief: with a contemplation to help access the antidote for yourself.

While there are currently seven generally accepted standard phases of grief (shock, denial, bargaining, guilt, anger, depression, acceptance), they do not always take place in chronological order. In addition, there is a great deal of individual variation in our progression. At times while mourning, we can experience the stages out of order, loop back to earlier stages, or somehow be feeling them all at the same the time. Because of the great suffering involved grief, we can easily become stuck in any phase.

The antidotes, or contemplations, at the end of each chapter allow us to keep moving, as well as to tap into the benefits that accompany each aspect of grief. The common theme to the antidotes is to bring clarity, or a greater perspective than just our thoughts or emotions. This often involves practices which distinguish between pain and suffering. Separating pain, an actual event, from suffering, how our mind/emotions react to the painful event, can help us move through great loss without getting stuck in any one place.

We do not need a belief system that coincides with the practices; all we need is an acknowledgement that there is a present moment and a sense of that presence inside us. The

keys to the antidotes to grief are an open mind and a willing-
ness, however small, to befriend difficult emotions long
enough to see what lies beyond them. We sit with the pain not
to make it go away, but to move through the experience fluidly, mining the gifts offered in every phase. The contemplations
and the gifts re-frame our understanding and provide a foundation for us as we move through challenging experiences in
our life.

This is a book about the trauma experience. As we look
more deeply, it becomes apparent that the experience of great
loss, or the breakdown of life as we know it, follows a similar
arc to the experience of a spiritual breakthrough. In sudden
loss, there is a traumatic event, a moment where the sky opens
up, disintegrating life as we knew it. Everything falls apart, and
nothing makes any sense. For a period of time we may try in
vain to return to the unconsciousness in which we lived- to the
way it was before.

A period of disorganization follows, which takes different
forms for each one of us, where we sort through what remains. The struggle to understand can lead to a spiritual ques-
tioning which deepens our connection with all life. This period
of disorientation, which is often the most frightening aspect of
grief because it ungrounds us so thoroughly, is the one that is
laden with unbelievable potential for allowing us access to
deep and lasting unshakeable happiness.

Eventually, there is reintegration, a re-forming of ourselves, where we begin to connect with life again with a greater
richness that comes from the very real sense of life's preciousness and precariousness. We start to rebuild our life in a new
way as we absorb this loss, and, hopefully, its resulting but unexpected gifts, into our lives. We would not wish our loss on
anyone, but we do value, and might not trade, the insights and
experiences that resulted because of it.

Along with trauma, the arc of this story is also one of spiritual journey and breakthrough- an experience of unity and recognition of true nature (which occurred for me in the wake of the most painful experience I could imagine). This is a moment *"where all your conditioning falls apart and nothing remains".* [1] On the spiritual path, this is followed by a period of disorder in which we are struggling to find a new foundation. In the words of the poet Rilke, we are *"standing on fishes"*. At times we may even be scrabbling backwards, trying to find solid ground. Like grief, this also includes a period of disillusionment and disconnection. In the Buddhist tradition, this is referred to as *getting stuck in detachment*. Finally comes embodiment, or regrounding: coming back into deep connection with present life, with greater consciousness and an ever-deepening sense of gratitude and compassion for all life.

Think of this as a spiritual self-help book for the bereaved. Amidst profound pain, it offers a way to embrace the spiritual journey that grieving provides, allowing us to move through the experience with fluidity and flexibility. Working with pain is powerful medicine which offers an antidote to the very thing we thought we needed to avoid. Ironically, the antidote to the poison of suffering occurs by befriending it.

Grief is a sacred experience. When we encounter difficulty is the most precious opportunity on life's path. Becoming intimate with pain can be a doorway to complete transformation of our being. There is a larger purpose to our grief. It is not just about getting through this difficult time, but about laying a foundation for getting through all difficult times. When we become intimate with our pain, we develop compassion, wisdom, and grace. We are able to move forward in peace and with power, not despite what life handed us, but because of it.

* * *

PROLOGUE

Imagine if you will, a scene in nature- an exquisitely beautiful Indian summer morning on the banks of a small river in rural Virginia. The early sun is fragmented into diamonds on the gently rippling surface of the moving water, which laps quietly at the shore in an irregular but rhythmic beat. Other than this, it is so quiet that you can almost hear the sound of the wind through the trees on shore, can definitely hear the wingbeats of the shorebirds as they fly overhead.

As you are watching, immersed in all of this peace, you turn your eyes toward shore to see an expansive green lawn with many old oak trees encircling a house on the shore- a magnificently proportioned, large whitewashed brick house with sunny terraces on either side and climbing roses at the entrances. It all looks so perfect- a feast for the eyes. As you follow the outline of the house you can see through the floor to ceiling windows to an inviting opulence inside- richly hued curtains, antique silver, ornate china, old books, and Persian rugs. This is a life you would love to step inside of, just for a moment, to know how it feels to live in such a way.

Toward one end of the house there is a huge bow window, shimmering in the sun. As you look through it you can see the outline of a tall woman inside her bedroom, and then the light begins to play upon the old leaded glass in such a way that when you look in, it is almost as if for a moment it becomes a portal into her entire world.

What you see is amazing. As in a movie, you are watching the images of her life. This is a woman who seems surrounded by absolute good fortune. You see a handsome husband of forty-four years; four beautiful, healthy, successful girls, all married with families of their own; a summer house- a family compound where everyone gathers each year. You glimpse family money- a comfortable amount of wealth with no need to work; friends and parties under the huge summer sky; family vacations and exotic travel- sailboats in the Caribbean, camels in India, elephants in Vi-

etnam; and eight happy blooming grandchildren gathered around her, smiling and laughing with her. It is almost too much to behold. There is so much bounty, and so much joy, too, in this one life. Here is one of the truly lucky.

You hear a sound nearby from the terrace off of the bedroom, and your vision zooms in on a bird's nest tucked into one of the rose bushes- you can see the almost grown babies squirming inside- and as you do the door just under it opens onto the side terrace. The mother bird flies away quickly as the woman walks out onto the warm brick terrace and descends the steps onto the lawn. Who is this lucky woman, to be in the midst of all of this beauty, to somehow be able to call it hers?

She is heading out toward the water, dressed in a red and black wool overshirt to protect against any fall chill in the air. Her lean legs walk slowly, a bit unsteadily, but with purpose, out onto a pier at the water's edge. The dock is long, about 200 feet, and there is an open-air boathouse at the end, on top of which the giant sticks and twigs of an osprey nest lend a naturally thatched appearance to the roof. Your gaze follows the woman on her long walk- you cannot seem to take your eyes off of her- she somehow seems out of place in this scene of incredible beauty (she is not even looking around her, and yet her halting steps continue. Where is she going?). At last she reaches the little house, turns into it, and seats herself, not visible on the bench as you would expect, but on the ground in the corner, close to the water, legs crossed beneath her, under the protection of the roof. All is still accessible from this vantage point- the gentle breeze, the waves against the boathouse, the sounds of the birds, the surrounding silence. The beginning of another impossibly beautiful day.

The woman takes a firm hold of something you now realize she must have been holding in her hand all along. She places the metal handle between her thumb and forefinger and anchors it in her mouth, angling it upward. Time stops for a moment, and nothing is happening. Then, in the next moment, which seems both infinitesimally brief and at the same time to go on forever, many things occur at once. You, the watcher, suddenly realize what is about to happen, but before you can even begin to raise

*your hand in a gesture that might indicate a stopping, before you can inter-
fere or change anything at all, the woman squeezes the trigger of the gun,
resulting in a huge burst of sound and fury that erupts in the face of the
moment. Gulls flap madly in alarm overhead. A nearby heron roused
from its feeding ground onshore squawks and takes rushed flight. The
sound reverberates in an echo up and down the tree filled
shoreline. It is as full as it can be. And then just as suddenly, everything
is silent again, and all is illuminated in the moment- everything and nothing at once.*

Now imagine this woman was your mother.

PART ONE:

WHEN THE SKY OPENED UP

1

SHOCK

*In the middle of the road of my life I awoke in a dark wood
where the true way was wholly lost.
~ Dante Alighieri (The Divine Comedy)*

THE STORY

I remember the day of my mother's death in a series of especially distinct instants. I remember a perfect Indian summer morning, immersed in the northeastern shoreline (on errands to help in the set up of a volunteer event). The sun glittered like stardust on the water, which gently slapped against the pier. The trees, yellow and orange and red, were aflame on shore. The sound of boat rigging played musically against masts in a gentle symphony.

I remember being in the parking lot of the farmer's market, my friend and I picking out table decorations for a benefit, when my phone rings. It's my husband and he is attempting casual, wondering when I will be home, but the sound of tension in his voice is instantly alarming. Though he would like to wait until I have driven home, I make him tell me what is wrong right away.

It is your mother. She is dead, he says. *How? What happened? I don't know,* my husband keeps saying, but I find I can't stop asking because I know there is an answer. He finally responds. *She killed herself.*

Suddenly things get very distinct. It is almost as if I am watching a movie of myself. So many things are happening at once and I am intensely conscious of all of them. I look up at the bright sun and huge blue sky. I can feel the beauty of it deep in my being. At the same time I am aware that I am talking. I hear myself saying over and over into my phone *I can't believe she did this. I can't believe she did this!* I am angry at her. I am disbelieving. I look at my hands, holding the phone. There is a feeling of ice that begins in my fingertips and moves slowly up my hands and forearms, numbing them. I am watching myself go into shock. As a clinician, I find the symptoms intriguing.

In linear time, it would be hard to imagine how many single moments there are in a lifetime. Most of them lie unrecalled somewhere below our consciousness. How many moments, even ones of pure joy, have been forgotten? How does the mind decide which moments to hold on to and which ones to allow to fade away? These ones are etched in my cells: my husband's alarm; my conversational tone; my forearms going numb; the intensely blue sky; watching it all happening like I was someone else. I *am* someone else.

Somehow, the friend in the car with me has left, and I am on the phone with my older sister, Julia. Her teeth are chattering, as she tells me how it happened. *She sh-sh-shot herself.* I envisaged the method even less than I expected the suicide, which I had foreseen even less than her death. Julia seems to think it imperative that I get home immediately. I can't see the rush to anything at all, but I begin to drive.

I move toward home. The sky is tremendous. It's sunny, and there are streaks of white across it. It feels achingly beautiful. As I look up at it, I hear the small voice of a child deep within myself. *It's okay...You're okay...It's fine....She's okay...Oh my god Mommy Mommy...why did you do this...*I am talking to my mother in the sky. *Oh you poor thing...you poor thing...It's okay now...You're okay...Don't worry...everything is okay...*

I feel tears come forth, the beginning of panic. I breathe in. A part of me is aware that I can't lose myself just now. I have to drive. I have to watch the road. I look up at the sky

again, so immense, as if it has opened up and absorbed everything into itself. I am filled up by the space left behind. Road.
Hands on the wheel. Breath. The expanse of the infinite horizon holds the enormity of it all.

When I get off the highway I pull over to the curb for a
moment. I hear a wild sound, and then realize it is coming
from me. It is animal, pure instinct from deep within. There is
no resistance to it. Eventually it passes. I drive the rest of the
way home. I see my husband. He holds me. My body is shaking. I feel weak. I sit down.

* * *

There is no ground under my feet, which makes it seem
very natural to be in a plane. I am with my older sister flying
down to Virginia, a few hours later. I feel the space around me.
There is so much of it. I feel my hands. I feel my feet. I feel
the tissue in my pocket. I breathe. I see the Atlantic shoreline
sparkling below. Every few minutes a question passes through
my consciousness like a cloud across a blue sky- logistical
questions, about how to explain all of this to my six year old
son, about my estranged youngest sister- *who will notify her?*,
about who is with my father at this moment. All of these little
realities, flashing across my mind. And I continue to breathe.

I watch the landscape change and the rivers of the tide-
water come into view. It is impeccable, a perfect symmetry. I
can't seem to get over the radiance of the world as I see it
from above- the water, the shoreline, the trees. Something
about the juxtaposition of being above the earth when I my
life is in freefall adds to the intensity of the moment. I can feel
with my whole being the infinite beauty of this planet, this life.
By the time we land, darkness is spreading across the sky. The
day seems to have been endless and at the same time I feel like
it is just beginning.

I have never been in shock and it is different than I expected. There is a deep beauty to it. I find myself amazed that I can feel such peace in the midst of such raw pain. I am intensely awake. I don't have the numbness of emotion. I just have very few thoughts. Everything has become so simple. There is immense pain. There is limitless beauty. There is boundless love. I feel all of these things at once. I keep putting one foot in front of the other, walking through this. Somehow, despite the fact that this is beyond my worst nightmare, I don't want to miss a thing.

* * *

A GREATER PERSPECTIVE

I had been working with various mindfulness practices for a few years before my mother's suicide, and, miraculously, like grooves on a newly tracked road, they provided a way forward for me, propelling me into each next moment. Grounding my meditative approach were the two realizations that consciousness encompasses much more than just our thoughts, and that we encompass much than our suffering. Only now in hindsight do I realize how helpful these were to me- how invaluable this can be when dealing with any kind of trauma. I had some loose structure in which to approach this overwhelming event. It was something I had been teaching others, and now I was practicing under conditions of extreme adversity.

In my experience, there were the events from this watcher's perspective- these are beautiful, almost perfect, even in their pain. Then there was the me who processed it all. I found that the extent to which I could silently and compassionately witness all that I was going through from this non-personal perspective was the extent to which my pain was softened, allowing me to walk through with a kind of inner strength I did not expect, but which was exceedingly soothing to me. In a time when I had been completely unseated, mindfulness practice gave me the only place to rest that made any sense at all.

The following contemplative practice got me through the first few weeks of shock. I still practice it in many moments throughout the day, in order to shift my awareness instantly from my thoughts and worries to the present moment. That it had become somewhat of a habit was invaluable to me in these initial days following mother's suicide. I felt my hands, I felt my feet, I kept my eyes open, and I breathed.

The fact that I was able to practice or sit still at all is a tribute to **the first gift of grief: it brings the blessing of shock, where our mind is quieted and our body is calm, so that we can hold the enormity of sudden change on our lives.** Because of the shock, I was able to access and inhabit the space left by the loss without being terrorized by it. Because my mind had slowed down and I experienced very few thoughts, I was not stuck trying to accommodate a story that was simply too overwhelming to make any sense of.

While my hands and forearms remained icy and numb for quite some time, my mind felt a degree of peace that could hold the enormity of the pain. The mind literally shut down to anything superfluous, so that while I could feel the pain of what had happened, it was not confused with the tremendous suffering my mind might have created from it had it been more active. There was a calm about all of the events over the next few days, as if linear time plodded quietly along but the whole concept of past and future no longer applied.

Every death, no matter how expected, is accompanied by some sense of shock. Even if we had been preparing for the loss of someone for many months, when the day comes that they are suddenly gone, the enormity of it is simply too much for us to absorb at once. Shock is a great protection to us in the first days of grief. One effect of it is that we all have particular access to the connection with the inner energy field of the body during this initial phase of grief, providing us with essential grounding during a time of upheaval.

* * *

ANTIDOTE TO GRIEF
1. Grounding in Inner Body Awareness: An Antidote to Trauma/Shock

INNER BODY CONTEMPLATION

Bring your awareness to your right hand. Feel the energy field of the right hand. What sensations do you feel (tingling, energy, your pulse, blood pumping through you)? Notice the breath as it causes parts of your trunk to rise and fall naturally. Notice your hand. Breathe into your hand. Can you feel the breath in your hand? Now bring your awareness to your feet. Breathe into your feet. Notice how they feel. Become aware of the greater intelligence at work in the body. The body's intelligence exists beyond our understanding and it keeps going despite our lack of attention toward it. We can notice our form and our form's reaction to that noticing. It may wake up or certain parts may feel dull. Don't judge the sensations. Just feel them.

Allow any thoughts to be there, but continue to return your awareness to each part of the body. Continue your focal awareness at different points- ankles, calves, knees, thighs, hips, stomach, heart, shoulders, arms, hands, neck, head. Notice differences in each area. As you tune into the trunk of your torso, notice the breath as it rises and falls, as it interacts with each area. This is not about making the whole core feel great. It is about simply feeling what sensations are present in your makeup right now. Next time it will be different. Now focus your awareness on the entire energy field of the body at the same time. Beginning with the feet, "run" your awareness up and down the body in a wave. Notice how it feels. As you open your eyes, keep some attention on the inner form.

Every moment that you keep some of your awareness on the inner body, you hold a state of consciousness that is beyond the thinking mind. Each instant that you do this, you allow the light of conscious awareness to grow stronger within you. It is like a flame to which you hold something incendiary: it grows stronger even if it does not start out burning at full force.

2

THRUST INTO THE PRESENT MOMENT

The deeper that sorrow carves into your being the more joy you can contain.
~ Kahlil Gibran

~

... Your eyes eventually open again as the sound and fury disperse, and as you look into the boathouse, you see the woman there, slumped in the corner, head down. It is almost as if she is asleep, or passed out, but her eyes are open, as if in surprise, and you see the small gun in her lap, and the blood behind her head. It is clear there is no life left in her. For a while it seems that time has stopped. There is only this silent field of stillness. Nothing is moving but the water beneath the dock, the trees swaying on shore, an occasional bird moving across this large sky. You remain completely absorbed in this backdrop, who knows for how long. Eventually, from your reverie, you hear footsteps on the dock and see police materialize, inspecting the scene. For a period things seems to go on like this- people wandering up and down the dock, gathering at the end of it, moving to and fro without much purpose or activity. The only clue to the movement of time is the sun moving across the sky. Then at some point, it seems like there is a forward motion to life again, as the police begin to remove what is left of her body...

THE STORY

When we get to my parents' house in Virginia, the deep, fall darkness outside seems to seep into the library, where we sit in shadow on big red couches. My bones feel as if they are submerged in ice, but I am warmed by the presence of my father and two sisters, Miranda and Julia. We try to piece together the details of what exactly has happened in the last twenty four hours. At first we start with the actual event, but this leads us back to when it all began.

My mother had been in a major depressive breakdown, the first one of her life, or so I believed, for the past 7 weeks. It had been increasingly stressful for all of us and we had been in close contact throughout. My father felt helpless and exhausted from constant care. My sisters and I had been trying to help from afar. We planned trips down there, but my mother had held us at bay, not wanting us to see her so debilitated. We were all still trying to wrap our minds around her unexpected, unpredicted breakdown. None of us can seem to make the jump from there to the reality that she is dead. The explosion of the gun with which she shot herself this morning has propelled us forward in time with such a momentum that we can't keep up.

My father says that these last few weeks she would ask him to come in and sit with her while she lay in bed. *If you're going to read, don't do it at the other end of the house- come do it in here.* She would lay there, eyes closed or crying and he would hold her hand, reading beside her. *You took the best care of me that anyone could have,* she said to him last night at dinner. *Last night!* he realizes. *She was saying goodbye to me!* He was awakened later in the night- she had fallen down in the bathroom and couldn't get up. She was drunk. He was angry. *I've been drinking,* she wept. *When did you start again?,* he asked fiercely. *This summer.* He brought her back to bed. He hugged her. *We'll get through this together,* he said. The last words they spoke.

The night is ever darkening, and my father takes his broken self to bed, the same bed which still holds my mother's body imprint on the pillow, which carries her scent in the sheets. My two sisters and I sit for a few moments, looking at one another. Then, almost without speaking, it is as if we are all aware of wanting to do the exact same thing. We must go out to the boathouse. We are compelled by the need to see what is left of our mother.

One of us finds a flashlight, another grabs a candle and matches, and we head out into the darkness, walking across the wet, cold lawn. We march slowly, unremittingly, the same steps she took, to the end of the dock. She would have known they were her last. We are walking in the view she awoke to every morning from her bedroom window, only now it's all darkness and shadows.

A huge bird, a heron, jumps out from the end of the pier and flaps away squawking. The moon is full in the October sky, moments from a total eclipse. We turn the corner into the boathouse, expecting to see her sitting there just as my father found her this morning; cross legged in the corner, looking out at the water, somewhat surprised, alive?, but head slumped just so much, and upon closer inspection, a small gun shadowed in her lap. *Peace is coming. Peace is coming soon. I can't see it now, but I know it is before me.* Is this what she was thinking, to have had the misdirected courage to do such a desperate thing?

We light the candle and place it on the ground in the cor- ner- the last place she sat. In the dim but powerful light of candle and moonlight we sit looking for bits of our mother. Clothes, hair, blood, bullets, gun.

I imagined things would be messier, and I am somewhat comforted to see that they are not. I can see where her head lay, still warm, just this morning. A small amount of blood has dried on the bench, a clear shiny trickle running down the cor- ner; some stray pieces of her hair; one very tiny piece of debris mixed in something that looks like a patch of hairless skin- like the fair skin of a baby inside the womb.

Amazingly, tonight is a full lunar eclipse, and some kind of planetary convergence, the significance of which has been in the news all week. We sit in the boathouse and watch as the brilliant full moon becomes eclipsed by the earth's shadow. We talk about our mother; what we would have wished for her and what things were. There are few words and there is no urgency to what we say. It is as if the force of our individual lives has come full stop, overshadowed by the gravity of the global activity surrounding us.

After awhile, we are drawn away from what is left of my mother and toward the moon. Emerging from the boathouse we sit at the end of the dock, looking up at the night sky. The eclipse has made the night anomalous: everything has a sharp focus but all the edges are simultaneously blurred in their own close shadow, and the sky casts a russet hue onto the pier. The moon looks as if it has a human bite taken out of it. It is a part of nature and yet seemingly outside of it. The stars in the clear sky are orange and pink and brown, like water passed through iron pipes.

In the magnetic pull of this moment there is no choice but to feel intimately connected with life and the greater plan of everything. It all feels beyond our understanding but supremely connected, interwoven in a complex pattern as brilliant as the moon itself and beyond; so bright it is almost inabsorbable. I can feel this whole commanding reality contained in the moon- the energy of its shadow, calling her home.

The heron continues to squawk. It is close by on the shoreline, flying back and forth from one side of the dock to the other. When I finally catch a glimpse of it, it is awesome, its rich blue color deepened by the grayish cast that shadows everything. We all feel with certainty that it is our mother, and it stays with us for quite awhile. It is all her- the bird watching over us, the moon, her blood, her skin, my sisters, me.

And there we are, the three of us, gathered around this great sky, the earth shadowing the moon, the sun hidden behind the earth, everything fine and indistinct at the same time. The air moves horizontally back and forth, like the rocking movement of a boat on water. Things feel incredibly sharp, and penetrated with a grayish cast as they are just before the start of a summer rainstorm.

Now a memory flashes through my mind. I am a child, and it *is* right before a rainstorm. It is afternoon, and we are all rowing in the Maine harbor. I feel the proximity of my sisters in the seat next to me, all crowded together in our bright orange life preservers, and I am enveloped in the safe presence of my parents. The sky suddenly darkens and the air becomes sharp and electric. Static fills the air, and our hair begins to stand on end. *Peter, for God's sake, row!* my mother says, petrified, and my father is rowing for the dock as fast as he can as the thunder rolls in and I feel the fear filling up the boat.

At the height of the eclipse, shadow presses on my eyes like a headache so that looking out feels like a great weight, heaviness squeezing my crown and brow, and yet my mind feels greatly expanded. I am dying to turn away but I don't want to miss an instant and somehow I want it to last forever. All the wisdom of the world, the pain and the beauty, is contained in this moment. It is a full state of luminosity. As the eclipse becomes total, the sky goes dark, and we look back at the house. At that moment, as if in response, the light in my parents' bedroom goes out, and we are in total darkness.

* * *

A GREATER PERSPECTIVE

As I went through these days, the fact that I was in shock helped me to drop all resistance, or disbelief, in what was occurring and had occurred. In every day life, I am a person who finds myself fighting with truths I don't like, as if that could somehow change the truths themselves.

Miraculously, with my mother's suicide I had no desire or extra energy to fight what was. This helped to keep the event clear of added layers of suffering that could have accumulated had any of us tried to make a more pleasing or different story out of it than what it really was. I continue the practice of allowing to this day when I encounter areas of resistance both small and large.

In this state of shock, resistance was impossible. It would have been akin to falling out of an airplane and trying to cling to the sky on the way down. It was so clear that I was in free-fall that I did not even bother to try to hold on.

The beautiful thing about this was that it gave me a glimpse of what it would be like to live in complete surrender. In a place of nonresistance, I experienced what I can only describe as a kind of major spiritual epiphany. The enormous amount of space that was left by my mother's sudden death allowed for an experience of true recognition. While I experienced other spiritually connected moments during my mourning, this was unlike anything I had yet or have since encountered in my life. It was an experience of unbelievable clarity and connectedness, made more powerful by the fact that it was happening in the midst of the deepest pain.

Thus, we encounter **the second gift of grief: it offers us moments of great clarity and spiritual wonder by connecting us to the present moment.** No matter what kind of loss we experience, with all grief comes some degree of shock. Our regular resistance to the flow of life is lowered, and we have access to moments of magnificently sharpened perception which result in a kind of euphoria. In the midst of the deepest pain, we can be opened to and allow an exquisite and unexpected beauty that comes with the mystery that is great loss.

Allowing contemplation is one way to help access this gift. It is the antidote to the common feeling of incredulity, or disbelief, that accompanies any death. As our mind tries to catch up to the present moment and we accustom ourselves to our new circumstances, we can make contact with a sense of connection to this moment and the depth and wonder that it encompasses through the simple act of surrender.

* * *

ANTIDOTE TO GRIEF
2. Allowing: An antidote to disbelief

ALLOWING CONTEMPLATION

Concentrate on this very moment and the world that lies within it- the sounds, sensed movement, sensations. Don't name them, just sense them. Be the observing presence of this moment as it unfolds. Relax into not knowing without jumping into thoughts about what is coming next. Allow your thoughts to be there, but don't judge them- don't become attached to them or lost in them. There is nothing you can add to this moment by interpreting it.

Create space around the thoughts. Any time you feel any kind of constricted energy, or trying, relax into it- allow it to be there, but create space around it. Relax into the space in which this moment happens. If you like, bring awareness to an area of discomfort in the body. Allow it to be there. Become intensely conscious of how it feels. Allow some space around the feeling. Soften into it.

What physical sensations do you actually feel? Allowing creates a bubble of gentleness around whatever it is we feel. It softens our experience of the moment. How much can you allow things to be *exactly* as they are, without focusing on how you would like them to be? Often, our resistance to a situation creates as much or more pain than the event itself. How much can you yield to rather than oppose the flow of life?

3

NATURE

It is not what you look at, but what you see.
~Henry David Thoreau

THE STORY

The next night, I wander through their house, absorbing the resplendence, trying to take in what has happened to my mother and to all of us, and hoping to soak in what is left of her. My parents built this dream house several years ago after a lifetime of imagining it. Throughout my childhood, they would sit and endlessly plan what they called "The Hunt Memorial Library"- the central room which would hold my father's vast collection of antique books, which he had spent years cultivating.

The design of the house is reflective of my father- perfectly proportioned and full of lively interest. To walk through it is to experience firsthand how being in a truly well designed space can enhance one's sense of ease and wellbeing. The things inside it are purely my mother. A rich and full life speaks from every corner: warm, deep colors on the wall; the meticulously collected books in the library; the pictures of extensive travel and family; myriad journals and letters on the desk. It is a house you want to walk in for hours, letting your eye travel like a wandering stream from one compelling object to the next; the long silver letter opener on the mahogany writing desk, the smooth heavy crystal bear, the tiny birds eggs in glass on the round side table in the library. These are the objects of my childhood, so familiar and nostalgic.

The hallway is lined with giant blown up family photographs of our history together, as if it were still happening- beginning with the first Christmas card photo of four little girls running naked into a secluded lake in Maine, and moving down the wall to each one of our weddings. I see photos of my mother smiling, laughing, and tan; us as children, teenagers, and adults; all of the grandchildren; even pictures of my estranged youngest sister, as if she was also still with us.

I walk into my mother's room. Her bed is unmade. I can see where her head lay on her pillow, and the mark her body left on the mattress. I can smell her lotion on the sheets. Did she put it on last night, part of an old familiar self-care routine? Would she have been able? Her silk robe is laid out on the chaise lounge. One pillow is on the floor, the one she always hugged when she slept.

The scene looks so ordinary, but in light of the new twisted truth it feels horrifying as well: the scene of the murderer before she commits the crime. I am both repelled and morbidly curious. Added to this is my realization that this most recent, intimate place she inhabited is my last, closest sense of my mother, temporary and already fading, and I am filled with a visceral sense of dread. I find a hair on the pillow, and take it- the last real piece of her. But I can feel that it is ephemeral, disintegrating even as I hold it in my hands. I sense a desperate need to hold onto her, to understand her, to puzzle out what has happened and why.

On her bed, right where the covers lay open, as if it were some normal morning where she had been reading before she got up, is a book called "Home Before Dark". This is a daughter's memoir of life with her alcoholic father, the writer John Cheever. Though we never discussed it, I knew it to be one of my mother's favorite books. What could this mean? Was this a message of some kind?

There is a second book, next to her bed; "Through the Mickle Woods", a children's book by Gregory Valiska with beautiful illustrations by Barry Moser. My mother had a great love of children's books and kept a large collection of them. This one is about a king who loses his wife, and the spiritual journey he takes to heal. While I know she was in no decent shape in her last few days, I don't believe in accidents, so I feel like in some way this is even the universe's note. There had to be some significance to the fact that these two books, which she had read and loved, were found so close to where she spent her final moments.

As I stand, afraid to move or change anything for fear of losing it all, the strong feelings running through me are felt through a veil of separation, almost as if they were happening to another person. I recognize again that they *are* happening to another person, for I am definitely no longer who I thought I was. A part of me is surprised that I have not expired from the enormity of this. I keep putting one foot in front of the other. The shock is protecting me from the full weight of what has happened, and I am still surprised to find myself actually moving through this with very little resistance.

I continue to walk through her bedroom, as if in a dream but in a state of complete wakefulness. The photograph of her when she was eight or nine years old in the little sleeping room off the main bedroom seems to carry a kind of foreboding. Were there fissures inside her then that would lead to her suicide, such a sad and lonely end? When did she see, finally, inside- *this is it- this is the end? My best years are behind me. My time has come.* At what point did she begin to see herself as more dead than alive? When did she know that she was truly about to die, and then by her own hand?

I sit at her desk. The chair smells like her perfume. I touch her beautiful stationary, the engraved kind where the initials are stamped out in the same color as the border. In the drawer there is a photograph, a panoramic of the early sunrise out front. It is exquisite- the sky and water are one- pink, yellow, and orange, with the dock and boathouse shadowed in black. *The boathouse where she killed herself this morning.*

The date and time are marked on the picture: 4:26am, last spring. I imagine her getting up out of bed to capture this incredible view from her bedroom window. She was awake in the early dawn hours, overwhelmed by the beauty of her surroundings, by the beauty of life. She wanted to catch that morning, to hold its magnificence. I am perplexed by these contradictory images of her, at once an innocent child of 9, a woman wanting to hold on to the sheer loveliness of a sunrise, and a deranged killer who shot herself in the head six months later.

In the top drawer of her bedside table I find my last letter to her, dated three weeks ago.

Dear Mom,

I hope you are feeling well- better than the last few weeks, and that things are on the upswing. There is nothing worse than feeling that low and I think the unfortunate thing about depression is that there is this stigma around it when it is nothing very different from having any other major medical illness, except that you feel so poorly both mentally and physically.

Please know that I am thinking about you and wishing you well. And when you are feeling very low, remember that it is just your mind playing tricks on you; that there is also another part of you underneath that that is much greater and stronger and continues to exist although you don't see it in the moment. The mind playing tricks may seem like a monster in the moment, but it is really only an insubstantial phantom that cannot prevail against the strength and beauty that is really you and exists beyond that.

That is the beautiful thing about family: that we all can see through to that part of you even when you don't see it yourself, and you can see it in us when we have forgotten it in ourselves.

We all love you very much and only and ever wish you the very best of life--and I'm sure it will get better! So hang in there and treat yourself gently-

Love, Leslie

* * *

A GREATER PERSPECTIVE

When I was grieving intensely, there were very few places which I felt could contain the enormity of my feelings. However, I could always count on the natural world. It reminded me of some much greater design. There was a strange comfort in the fact that even something as huge as my mother's suicide did not affect the cycle of nature- the moon and sun and the planets just kept going.

I found that when I was in a natural place, it brought me to a place of thoughtless awareness. I still find it is the easiest place to reach an awareness beyond my mind. It is such a human instinct to be deeply moved by the immensity and beauty of the cosmos. When you look closely enough, what place in untouched universe is not enchantingly beautiful?

It was nature that taught me compassion, acceptance, mercy, and forgiveness. The universe was this greater awareness. It existed in the present. It was life. I felt that greater force (as opposed to some vice or escapist thought or behavior), as the shelter for my suffering. Nature is the refuge, the container that can hold all of it. It has everything we need. Whatever we cannot handle, we can give over to it.

Nature allows us to see the cycles of life and death. Fully grieving a particular loved one allows us to see the value of everything alive. We realize the death that is a part of every living thing. There billions and trillions of deaths that make our landscape possible, such as the snails, mussels, clams and other shelled creatures that form the sand on a rocky coastline. Without the cycle of life and death, we would not have stark winter landscapes, the rich earth from which new plant life springs, or the brilliant fall leaves of an Indian summer. The universe is a constant interplay of life and death, and this is what makes it so engrossing.

When in intense mourning, we have access to the cosmos- a force greater than our own comprehension- in a new and different way. Feeling completely overwhelmed by great loss offers us the opportunity to rely on an intelligence greater than our own mind. **The third gift of grief is that it connects us with something greater than our own mind: nature, which can gently hold the enormity of what we feel.**

* * *

ANTIDOTE TO GRIEF
3. Connecting with the greater force of nature: An antidote to feeling overwhelmed.

<u>NATURE CONTEMPLATION</u>

It is easier to enter the present moment while in a natural place, because a nature carries the vibration of all that is- it is not a product of our minds but exists outside of it. Spend five minutes sitting quietly in a natural setting. Allow yourself to experience the universe in thoughtless awareness, without naming what you are seeing. Tune into the greater intelligence at work in nature, and on the earth. Notice the sights and

sounds outside, quietly moving to their own rhythm: the animals, plants, and trees. Connect your aliveness with the aliveness in the rest of the natural world. Take in the cycles of
nature, gently moving with their own rhythm: the cycle of this
day, the cycle of the seasons, the cycle of the earth moving
around the sun.

Notice the innate surrender inherent in all plants, trees,
and animal life. Contemplate a tree- it has no worries; the
branches do not fight with one another; the leaves on a tree
are not concerned about their imminent death but fully em-
body their present reality. The plants and trees can hold the
enormity of all of life's pain, and pleasure. The birds are not
arguing with themselves. A cat does not have a worry about a
future moment. It deals with each moment as it arises.

Make it a point to access nature for five minutes a day.
Experience nature with quiet, non-naming attention. Just looking at an object in nature can bring you immediately beyond
the mind into thoughtless awareness.

4

KINDNESS

Courage is the mastery of fear, not the absence of fear.
~ Mark Twain

Dear Mom,
Today I took a bath in your big tub and I know you were the last person to use it be-
fore me and Dad cried and touched your face at the morgue. Is this really what you wanted to
have happen?

~

...The police have brought a stretcher out onto the pier, carefully lifted the
woman onto it, carried it down the long dock, and loaded it into their van. They
gather around the driveway, writing and talking on cell phones, finishing up
their business. In the midst of the activity, you notice a man there, quietly sitting
with the woman, holding her hand. He appears completely broken, hunched over
the back of the van, his face wan and expression sober. It takes a moment to
recognize that this is the handsome husband you saw in the earlier glimpse into
this woman's life, because he looks so different. It is as if all of the happiness
has completely drained out of him. He touches the woman's cheek with great
tenderness before her body is covered up and driven away...

THE STORY

My father and sisters and I sit in the great library together over the next few days, still trying to comprehend what has
happened to our family. That we are now on a singular journey
together becomes abundantly clear. It is like we all found ourselves on the other side of a secret door we weren't even sup-
posed to know was there. We did not want to find it, but now
we know something- we've witnessed something- and we can't
go back. We must stay together to find out the rest, no matter
where it leads. We have no choice.

We all express a determination that we as a family will survive this, if possible without becoming permanently devastated by it. We make a pact to stay open and walk through this fire of pain together, no matter how long it takes, and we promise one another that *no one will leave.* It is because of my mother and estranged youngest sister that we know with certainty that we will not abandon each other, for none of us wants to feel the pain of that again nor consciously inflict it upon one another.

* * *

A few days have passed, and everyone else has gone to bed. My mother's funeral is in the morning. I am wandering the dark hallways of the house in the quiet of the night, as I have since I arrived, searching for my mother.

As I inhabit the quiet of my grief, I am suddenly dumbstruck that she lied to me in such a profound way. I asked her more than once about suicide, and she said over and over that she never thought of hurting herself. I can see from her checkbook that she could not even write her name, the hand was too shaky, and yet she managed to get herself a gun and bullets. Her mind was all blackness, she said. She could not stand up, and rarely left the bed. Yet there was space to secretly plan all of it.

I thought about how I had gone to Italy to represent her at her niece's wedding only weeks ago- she could not make it. I was gone for ten days in the midst of her breakdown. I had called her to check in throughout, but I was an ocean away. I felt a panic at the thought of what I might have done instead with those ten days.

When I wake up the next morning I am confused. This story I am living is so unreal, and yet I keep waking up to it. The sunrise is incredible. The clouds are red against the boathouse. *What time did you wake up? Did you see a morning like this? So much peace but you couldn't reach it. Were you scared when you woke up or comforted? Was your hangover torturing you with guilt?* These clouds are unreal, hand painted by God. This backdrop of beauty stops the mind.

Last night I thought I felt her hand on mine. I am not sure whether it comforted me or simply made me afraid. My hands and arms are still so icy, into my bones. I wonder if they will ever be warm again. I miss her, and, ironically, I miss having my mother to process what I am going through right now.

My sister Julia dreamt about her. Mom called her on the phone. *Where are you?* Julia asked. *How can I reach you? How will I talk to you again? I am in a place where you can't reach me,* she replied. *There is no number here.* Miranda felt her presence in the house, too, and was frightened by it.

It is the day of the funeral. My sisters and father and I are at the labyrinth nearby to walk and collect ourselves for what is to come. This is the same labyrinth that my father was walking at the exact moment my mother pulled the trigger of the gun. He had joined a group that meditated there weekly, and it had become a habit to walk it on his own. He was on his way back from the dentist and had stopped off here. *She double-checked with me that I had a dentist appointment that morning!* my father remembers suddenly. *She confirmed the time with me that last night- it had been changed from Thursday to Wednesday, and she verified it again with me at dinner. She knew I would be out of the house! Oh God!*

We are alone and the vast sky is open. The usually almost incessant tape in my head is quiet I am somehow simultaneously filled with raw pain and permeated with peace. It is a precarious sense, as if it might disappear at any moment, opening the gates to let the waves of devastation come flooding in. As I walk, my mind keeps repeating a simple phrase that my sister Miranda shared with me, which helps my awareness to hold onto this delicate stability. *Keep your mind where your feet are.*

The labyrinth is set by the water, and as we each complete our journeys we walk off, finding private spots on the shoreline, distant from one another but close enough to feel the comfort of our connection. We have fallen through the sky into a new place. The present moment is holding all of it, and I am infinitely grateful for this, for I could never bear it on my own.

* * *

The rest of the family arrived yesterday- our children and husbands- and we are on the water again, some of us in kayaks, others of us on the dock. My sisters and I have washed my mother's blood away from the corner of the boathouse as best we could with bleach and scrub brushes- sweeping away the last bits of her. We have sat in that spot, seen the last view she saw at the same time of day. We have gone to the morgue and seen her head sewed back onto her body after the mandatory autopsy because of the gunshot wound- the forehead not quite right, the small vulnerable shoulders, skin still red from the cold storage drawer. She looked like my mother but somehow not: forehead too big, eyes closed, mouth in a grimace. I wanted to reach down and smooth her top lip over her teeth into her regular expression. Instead I touched her soft cheek, flushed and cold. She was not there.

The funeral home was hesitant to show us the body after the autopsy: they warned us we might be shocked. *Could we be in any more shock than we already were?* I wondered. We had to sit at a table where they passed us mints and made us sign some kind of waiver- *that we would not sue them if we didn't like her appearance?* I wondered.

The funeral director stayed in the room with us. He said something like, *If it is any comfort, I have some personal experience with these and they are not themselves.* I wasn't sure whether he was talking about suicides or dead bodies.

We have received her effects- things she had on her person when the police removed her after filling out their report and took my father's fingerprints before concluding the cause of death: self-inflicted gunshot wound to the head- a watch, her wedding band, and a single, bloodstained earplug. We were more fascinated by the man who delivered them than the effects themselves. The young son of the funeral home director did not seem cut out for this- too shy and vulnerable, his hands covered with white acid burns from the preservatives. *Had he chosen this life for himself,* we wondered? In my excessively sensitive state it seemed like I could feel his own deep secret pain.

On the dock it is sunny and warmed by the sound of running children on wood planks, looking for crabs in the traps along the pier (I am curious whether she recently put bait in them. She liked to use raw chicken). Several of us have kayaks out on the water. I have paddled out much farther than I normally would- I have reached what feels like the place where life meets death. It is as if I am on a movie set and have paddled past the drawn horizon and through the screened background, ripping right through the painted scene. Only as I go through this veil, instead of everything falling apart, the world and everything it contains expands into an unfathomable amount of space.

It is as if the sky has opened up and sucked up what I knew of life, and as I step through, I am transported into an understanding of everything so vast that I have been rendered immobile, dazzled. It is almost too exquisite to bear, the birds playing on the water's surface, the trees on the shoreline, the perfect silence, the infinite symmetry, and space holding all of it with ceaseless tranquility.

* * *

Crowds of people are spilling out the back of the church as we arrive for the funeral. Chairs and speakers have been set up to accommodate them, but there is not enough space. As I approach, my feet abruptly stop moving, and I am frozen in place. I do not want time to move forward in this way. I do not want to be going to my mother's funeral. Suddenly it is all too devastating. *Keep your mind where your feet are*, I hear in my mind, like a mantra. I look down. And as I repeat the phrase, I find that my steps are no longer held back and I am able to enter the church, holding the hand of my sisters, my husband and son close behind. I feel eyes on me. I see the incredible flowers that her friends have arranged. I sit. My father gets up to speak.

There is not much to say about something like this. I want to thank everyone for the numerous thoughts, cards, and gestures. Someone once described this church as simply a community of people who love each other. Never have I felt that more than these last few days. People who have come today, have called, stopped by the house, written, or dropped food- we have felt that caring so immensely and we thank you. Barbara loved this community and she would have loved seeing you all.

Barbara's death comes after a terrible struggle. She went through great torment in the last weeks of her life, and I think I loved her more during those moments when she was most ill than I ever have. Even in the depths of her illness she never lost her caring for certain things- her children and grandchildren- she loved them more than anything. They were the most important thing to her...I hope she's found peace.

I look out the large window behind the altar. It is filled with a warm bright light, and as the music of the hymn plays I can see the sun shining onto the fall leaves in the trees outside.

I am filled up with it. It is peace. It is her, as if she is just out-side the window, looking in, so close right now, so infinite. I can feel all of her shining through the glass. I want to hold on-to this so desperately, but I know it is useless. I can already feel her leaving, and it is an exquisite pain to know that she will on-ly be moving farther away from me with each moment.

After the funeral, the warmth of people is filling up the space she has left behind. There is food and the sweet scent of flowers and the humming noise of connection in the air. The children are playing on the swings outside, and it feels like eve-ry inch of space inside is filled with love.

* * *

A GREATER PERSPECTIVE

As the first few days after my mother's death passed, and more people came into this new world we were inhabiting, it took on a reality at times that I found myself incapable of moving through with ease. Our walking meditation in the laby-rinth on the day of the funeral was what I referenced in order to keep moving through an experience, one footstep at a time, that I thought might at times crush me. It boiled life down to its most very basic actions: Keep your mind where your feet are. Keep one foot in front of the other. Breathe. Walking meditation can be done with or without a labyrinth. You can set your own, regular path.

As I kept my mind on the moment before me, I found much more than suffering and devastation in my experience. I found an inexpressibly profound connection with my father and sisters at the labyrinth. As I kayaked, I found a deep con-nection with all life. In the midst of the deepest pain, I was opened to a beauty and mystery both exquisite and unex-pected. As I entered the church, I sensed an overwhelming outpouring of human love and goodwill from every person present.

The opening that grief creates can help us to see and welcome the unexpected kindnesses that come with grief. Sometimes it is only when we feel our most wretched that we can believe we deserve the kind of help that comes through human connection. This brings us to the **fourth gift of grief: it bonds us to the best of humanity by giving us access to deep human connection, kindness, goodwill, and love.** One way to access this treasure is by connecting deeply to the fullness of the present moment through walking contemplation. It can open us to one of the most valuable balms of mourning: deep human connection.

* * *

ANTIDOTE TO GRIEF
4. Walking Contemplation:
An antidote to a sense of devastation

WALKING CONTEMPLATION

As you walk, focus on the sensation as you place one foot in front of the other on the ground underneath you. Keep your mind where your body is, and become aware of the physical sensations in your feet, your legs, your hips, your heart, shoulders, and head. Notice the rhythm of your footsteps-constant, ceaseless.

Become aware of the rhythm of your breath in each moment- the life moving through you as you move through life. Notice the rhythm of it and the music it makes with the rhythm of your footsteps. Footsteps are moving you, and your experience is changing with each step, but the constant is the steps that keep happening, the body that moves, and breath that flows through you. Now notice the rhythm of the moment around you. Notice the fullness of the moment, so abundant but constantly changing. Attentively listen to and watch each aspect as it happens, so you don't miss anything. Let your steps be the anchor for the constant change in life: rich, plentiful, painful, and mysterious.

PART TWO:

WAKING UP
(DISORGANIZATION)

5

SELF BEYOND THE STORY

To go in the dark with a light
is to know the light
To know the dark, go dark
Go without sight
And find that the dark, too, blooms
and sings, and is traveled by
dark feet and dark wings.
~Wendell Berry, To Know the Dark

THE STORY

As I look back on these first few days, I am still surprised that I wasn't completely absorbed by the pain to the exclusion of anything else. I had so many moments of what I can only describe as universal peace. I felt a full sense of this awesome life the likes of which I had never known before. That is not to say that I did not feel amazing raw pain, but I was not lost in it. I expected that shock would be more numbing and less awakening. But with it I was somehow able to stay conscious as the watcher of my experience and so experience my pain in a less complicated way. There was a kind of softness to it, and though I did not intellectually understand it I could feel a larger context to it so that in the end it became almost sacred.

One of the other effects of the shock was that in my experience, the split between the thinking mind and the space around it became very pronounced. The absurdity of the intellect with its random thoughts was juxtaposed with the stillness and peace of the larger natural order. The mind seemed to me so obviously inferior, first and foremost because it was the mind that had led my mother to her untimely, self inflicted, violent death.

Over the next few days and months, as I began to come out of shock, I experienced both the worst and best moments of my life. I experienced pain, raw and pure, in its entirety: the pain of a mad world in which something like this could happen; the recognition that, like one of the billions of stars in the night sky, this was only one horror among just as many in the existence of humans on this planet; the feeling of common responsibility for such violence- that as a world, as a species, we have all somehow failed when we have created a world where people go so desperately astray. One some level we are all complicit in every crime, because we are here, and life is a mirror, and her pain or anyone else's is just an individual manifestation of our collective unconsciousness.

As the witness, I was equally as interested in my survival and how I would get through this as I was in how and why my mother did not survive. Those two streams ran parallel and together throughout the next year of my life. Also in the mix was my journey with my father and two remaining sisters as we walked through the rubble of our family history, trying to look at things with these new wide-open eyes.

When I returned from the funeral and re-entered my old life, I felt completely alien. Those moments when you wake up before the narrative of your day comes in- those moments were very long for me because the entire story of my life up to now had fallen away. When the story did come in, it was so new that I had to remind myself of what it was. Then the new facts and the pain attached to it came with a rush of feeling so strong that many days I just climbed back into bed from the weight of the emotion.

Grief takes unique forms for different people. In CS Lewis's book about his wife's death, A Grief Observed, he describes *a sort of invisible blanket between the world and me.*[2] I, on the other hand, felt completely exposed, like every time I left my house I was being bombarded by bright sunlight after years in solitary confinement. At times I experienced my grief as actual physical pain, and like an animal, raw and wounded, I wanted to curl up and protect myself from the elements until I could heal.

I had no resistance to anything, and there was nothing to hold onto: I had lost who I thought I was. The basis of my entire identity- the stories that I had told myself about my life and family- had fallen away and I was left completely bare. I just surrendered to those moments, because I did not seem to have a choice, and when I remembered, I would also practice a kind of basic gentleness toward myself and all that I was experiencing.

A part of me thought that I would still be able to carry on with my old life, but the return to anything like that was impossible. I had experienced the complete disintegration of the narrative of my life. My identity- the entire context of my life, had completely fallen apart. Without this, there was very little forward momentum anymore. This was isolating, because I was definitely traveling at a different pace than most of the people around me.

I did feel an impetus to re-interpret my entire past in light of this new event. There was also a continuing part of me that longed to return to the familiar landscape of my past. I craved a kind of comfort I hoped I might find there, but this was impossible. The past had betrayed me and the future was uncertain. Things seemed stalled in the present moment, and it became the only refuge.

There were times I fell into my pain and got lost there for a while. It was almost a relief, because without it I did not know who I was or how to be in the world. I would try and practice dropping the storyline of the desolation and just staying with the sensations in the body. And as I came out of these episodes there would be some recognition that I had been gone and had somehow returned again. I tried to forgive myself for needing some ground under my feet, even if it was a suffering ground.

For a period, I watched myself make an identity out of the sorrow. I derived a certain kind of gratification from being miserable. I went through a course of trying to feel as wretched as my mother did. I wanted to know what it would feel like to want to die so powerfully. I guess I thought that if I made sense of it, it would somehow make the pain go away. I thought it would complete my journey.

Trying to understand any one person is like trying to fathom the universe. It is an impossible, endless, depthless process. After my mother's suicide, we as a family spent a long time in this enterprise. I think somehow we knew that ultimately it was a fruitless search. We would never get certain answers from someone who was not with us. Everything we tried to do in this service would be speculative, a projection tinged with our own subjective interpretations.

On the other hand, we knew that looking under every stone was the only way to release the darkness that had invaded our family. We felt we had to revisit our history in order to gain a new perspective on it, because our old frame of reference no longer applied. We had to look at every painful thing that we had not wanted to see, every feeling we had stuffed away, every thing we thought might destroy us, so that we could once again remember the good things that had been shadowed by it.

This involved help from the skilled Dr. F, a sharp and talented family therapist, who my mother had seen briefly before she committed suicide. It also involved deep, direct emotional bonding with one another, a kind of first for our family. For me it incorporated the spiritual practice of meditation, in order to separate the many layers of my pain, its origins, and the suffering I experienced as a reaction to this pain.

The first of these painful truths was the bold fact that our mother had chosen to leave. There is no cure for this sense of abandonment other than to feel it, to sit with it. I cultivated a process of contemplation, elaborated on in Chapter Sixteen, which was extremely useful in this practice. It allowed for separating the actual pain from the personalization of it. This personalization is a common and unconscious reaction to most pain and amplifies it into a kind of inner agony.

Another obvious wound to look at was that we had not been able to prevent this. We had missed every classic sign she had shown. Never was this more apparent, aside from the actual moment I learned of her suicide, than when I put a list of the ten common characteristics of completed suicides in front of me (See Appendix IV) and in retrospect could see that she fit almost every sign.

Something else that took some time to see clearly was that this was not a darkness which had invaded our family recently, but one that had been there all along, building over generations to this awful crescendo. It was not as if we hadn't been aware of our dysfunctions before, but this event put things in a whole new light, leaving us cognizant that there was still so much we had to wake up to on this journey.

* * *

A GREATER PERSPECTIVE

I suspect that it was the effect of the shock and a sense of denial that is common to all grief, but from the moment of my mother's death, I seemed to be a witness to myself and my grieving process. This was not an unpleasant sensation, but rather helped me to look into places and bear pain that I thought I was incapable of sustaining. As the shock wore off, and I got lost in too many what-ifs, whys, and summations, I used a practice learned from Eckhart Tolle of *watching the thinker*. This involves consciously witnessing one's thought process as it happens, and recognizing the greater witness as a part of oneself.

I knew it was my mother's thoughts and perceptions that had cost her her life, so I was determined to detach from my thoughts when they became too much of a guiding force in mine. I found that this witness- this silent, compassionate presence- was my great friend. It was somehow me but greater than me at the same time. It allowed me a wider perspective on everything. It was compassionate and nonjudgmental.

One benefit that accompanies the common grieving phase of denial or disbelief, is that through it we can access a sense of objectivity, or separation from the narrative that we think defines us. Somehow, as the old story of who we are falls away and we experience a kind of denial of the new one (as one mourner put it, *it doesn't quite feel right*), we feel like an observer in our own life.

In her book, The Fruitful Darkness, Buddhist teacher and anthropologist Joan Halifax writes, *Our stories are our protectors, like our immune system, defending against alienation...they are the connective tissue between culture and nature, self and other, life and death, that sews the world together, and in telling, the soul quickens and comes alive.*[3] Despite this, having a part of our story suddenly fall apart can leave space for us to recognize how much more than it we really are. As we rebuild a new one, we can incorporate more than our history, more than our thoughts, into our sense of ourselves.

This **fifth gift of grief, a sense of separation from our story, allows us to experience our sense of who we are in new and expanded ways.** We step away from the common trap of having the stories in our lives be the story of our life. Rather than feeling this sense of separation as isolating, witness contemplation helps us to recognize this greater observer as a part of ourselves, thereby expanding our sense of who we really are.

* * *

ANTIDOTE TO GRIEF
5. Witness Contemplation:
An antidote to a sense of denial

WITNESS CONTEMPLATION

As you sit comfortably, allow whatever thoughts that come up to be there. Watch them as they happen. Notice the speed at which they happen, the intensity of some of them. Don't judge them- don't become attached to them or lost in them. Allow them to be there. Keep some attention on the space around the thoughts, in which they happen. Allow this space to soften your experience of the thoughts. If you find yourself fixed in one spot, on one thought or set of thoughts, just become aware of the thoughts again as they pass through your awareness like words across a blank computer screen. Who is doing the watching? A higher dimension of consciousness. This is who you really are-the mind is only a small portion of you. You are the background across which your thoughts move. As you go through the day, watch yourself. Be the larger awareness in which your actions and thoughts happen.

6

A DEEP WELL OF STILLNESS

Fanaticism is a frantic effort to keep one half of the truth at bay while the other half takes control. - Robert Johnson (The Shadow)

~

... As the police van takes the woman's body away, you approach again the large bowed window where you saw her this morning. It is open again, shimmering; as if you can you can see her life inside it once again. As you watch, you see that the woman is driving somewhere. She gets out at the local pawnshop and, moving rather slowly, walks with purpose inside. I'd like to buy a gun, you hear her say, 22 caliber. My husband travels a lot, and I'd like it for safety. The man behind the counter nods and shows her a small gun with a white ivory handle. He demonstrates how to use it. That will be fine, she says, I'll feel so much safer now. She completes the purchase politely, places the gun in her purse and leaves the store...

THE STORY

Several weeks after my mother's suicide, what is left of our family gathers once again at my parents' house in Virginia, to find comfort in one another and to begin the journey that we will continue jointly for the next year. As best we can, we re-trace my mother's footsteps, trying to make sense of what has occurred.

The first step is to see Dr. F, the therapist that my mother had just started seeing in the weeks before she killed herself. Though she only saw my mother three times, we hope she can shed some light on her and on the awful enigma she left behind. Dr. F will also help us take a painful look at some of the agonizing truths that we had missed about our mother, our estranged sister, and our early family life.

Suicide is rarely a sudden occurrence, she tells us. *It is far more often the result of a long, debilitating breakdown of an individual's emotional health.* We need help to see the truth of this; to separate the hard facts from the myths that we had told ourselves about our lovely but dysfunctional family. In the end, Dr. F will help us put what is left of our mangled, confused, grief sodden clan back together again.

My mother had been in a major depressive breakdown over the last seven weeks. As far as any of us could tell, this was nothing like anything she had ever experienced before. She had certainly had depressed or tough periods in her life. In the past few years, she had lost most of her hearing, and we had watched her become increasingly isolated as a result of it. Earlier in her life, she had even had alcoholic breakdowns, but this was different. The fact that she shared what was happening to her and how she felt about it was an indication of just how serious it was. This was a black hole that swallowed her up and she could not get free. There was no coming back from it. We all thought there was, and she had spared us the raw truth.

I am as confounded as you about what happened, Dr. F explains, but she is willing to look deeper with us. She says that Mom appeared very fragile and very afraid in their few sessions together. She had been in therapy one other time in her life for counseling with Dad, who reported that she hyperventilated through every session, so the sessions became more about managing the anxiety of her being there than they were about any kind of marital help. I wondered what awful truths she was so afraid of revealing about herself.

I think I am depressed, she had said in tears after a summer of completely out of character, passive disengagement in which she slept and isolated herself from everyone; a total departure from the tense angry spitfire of a mother I had become used to. Upon her return from summer vacation in Maine, she had gone to her doctor, told him that she thought she might be "a little depressed", and been prescribed some Prozac.

Within a week she went from walking and talking to fainting, blackouts, and being bedridden. She was still talking openly to us about her symptoms, which was extremely unusual for her, and we convinced her to approach the doctor about this sudden worsening of symptoms. When she did, she was given a callback from an office nurse, who told her not to worry about it, so she dutifully kept taking the medication for two more weeks, hoping for a change. *I feel like I am being poisoned,* she said. The lack of response increased an already acute mistrust in doctors. After three and a half weeks on Prozac, she called the office again and was placed on Lexiprau- again by a nurse, the doctor not having seen her in person or talked to her since the first brief visit.

She could not get out of bed- everything felt so painful- she said she would just lay there and try not to think. She would lose consciousness, fall down, throw up, and could not eat. Mornings were worse than afternoons, but by evening, she was able to eat a small meal with my father. *When you are in that place, where there is such darkness, is there any sense of perspective, a reminder to yourself that this will pass, and get better, as it does each evening?* I asked her at one point. *When I am in that place, I can't see anything. I have no perspective,* she responded. *There is nothing but blackness.*

What a terrible place of pain she was coming from, mused Dr. F. *For a woman as you describe, how desperate for relief she must have been and what courage it must have taken to even walk through my door.* In their first session, Dr. F asked for her trust. *Sometimes the right dose of medication can take a few weeks to sort out. But I am asking you to trust me- to stay with me until we can sort the medication out together. You will feel better. But you will have to trust me until you do. Can you do that?* My mother agreed that she could, and even sounded somewhat hopeful. She was immediately prescribed a new anti-depressant- Wellbutrin. I remember she certainly sounded hopeful to me in our phone conversation right after she saw the doctor. *She was so kind,* she had said.

In the meantime, we were all watching (and listening to) our mother unravel and our sense of utter powerlessness was anguishing. My father was overwhelmed. The attempt to find a psychiatrist in a small rural southern town had been exhaustive. Even when he finally found one, it had been difficult to get her to agree to go. He had also been unsure if she could physically make it. He saw the worsening situation increasingly moving toward hospitalization, but knew well that this was her worst fear, and so was unsure how this might look. Could he really hospitalize her against her will? How would he even get her there? The whole thing was so foreign to him and he felt unequipped to handle it. I think we all did.

My mother refused any idea of in person visits, saying she couldn't stand for us to see her like this. We planned one anyway: some of us would go down there and give my father respite and us a chance to be with her and assess the situation in person. Unfortunately, things happened so quickly that we never got the chance for this visit to occur.

Four weeks in, she spent most days in the fetal position in bed for the most part unable to speak. At times on the phone, she was perplexed. *I shouldn't be feeling this way. There is no reason for it. I have a great life. I have everything.* Other times, she could barely get words out for sobbing, and she just kept saying over and over, *I don't think anyone can help me, I don't think anyone can help me . . .* It was like witnessing an animal suffer-- she had so few defenses, and whatever was happening to her was so incomprehensible that it was difficult for her to articulate. That she appeared to be moving quickly toward hospitalization was, on the one hand, worrying as it was her worst fear (she was beyond terrified of all medical environments), but on the other hand, we hoped, it might be a small relief because she was in such agonizing pain and so desperate for relief that it might be some comfort to at least give that pain up to someone else, whoever it was.

My sisters and I all had our own reactions to the worsening situation. Julia's response was utter empathy. Despite a long and tangled relationship with our mother, it was literally tearing her heart out to hear her suffer so deeply. Being a person of action in a crisis, she was busy calling hospitals, finding therapists, and offering concrete help to my father. Miranda, in her usual compassionate way, was talking to my mother several times a day, drawing from her not small arsenal of emotional tools to try to help her access any kind of emotional relief.

My response was more complex. When I was with her on the phone, I could be present to her great pain and try and offer what I could in the way of immediate soothing and some hopeful path or outcome to hold onto. When not with her, I was angry with her. I was frustrated with my father. I felt hopeless about her situation. A part of me couldn't see her coming out of this. *What do you expect when you bottle it all up for sixty four years*, I thought. I was discouraged trying to help someone who so many times over the years had refused to help herself. I felt like I was banging my head against the wall.

As a clinician, my sense of hopelessness should have been a conspicuous warning sign to me. In therapy, one way to tell if a client is truly depressed is that you will feel depressed when in any kind of contact with the client or contemplation about their case. In the case of my mother, I had missed everything. I was crushed by the weight of this knowledge.

At the end of their second session, Dr. F tells us, my mother was still hopeful about the drug working, though she had not seen any lessening in symptoms. She was switched to Paxil. By the third session, she appeared to be putting a small bit of trust in Dr. F, and as the session was ending, Dr. F expressed hope that this medication would work. *I hope it doesn't work, too!,* said my mother fervently. Dr. F attributed this bizarre response to the mental confusion that can come from such a deep depression. Looking back in this new light, though, we saw it differently. *She had already bought the gun,* Julia commented. Was an unconscious part of her hoping that it would not work so she could carry out this new, more immediate plan for relief? How long had she been planning this suicide anyway?

As we go over them, the signs are so obvious. She was clearly desperate- she had said as much. She was relying solely on a cure (medication) that was not working. She was petrified of doctors, and heading toward a hospitalization as a last resort. Why couldn't I see what was happening- what was going to happen to her? Was it just too painful? With all these facts before me, what I wonder now is how could this not have happened.

To look at this, to be with these truths as a family, was excruciating. To continue on in this way would require a complete breakdown and re-ordering of the story we had each told ourselves about our family. *A formidable task,* Dr. F called it, *which requires much bravery.* This was our journey of the next year, and she was one of the angels who guided us through.

* * *

A GREATER PERSPECTIVE

I could see that my mother's lifetime pattern of pushing away what was painful to her in whatever way she could was what led her, eventually, to murder her self. My sister Miranda said that she looked at the suicide as my mother *murdering her mind*, which had become untenable. I believe that by killing herself she found a misguided way to, quite literally, *kill her pain*. From this perspective, it became imperative to me personally to find a better way to manage strong emotions.

I could see that the stakes of pushing away our suffering, not being patient with it and moving through it to find perspective, are extremely high, not only for ourselves but for the world. Think of the mass shootings that take place regularly in our world. What is it that the killer can no longer manage? His pain. He has lost perspective. His emotions have become so overwhelming that he will resort to taking lives, including his own, in order to appease them. When seen from this perspective, there is no doubt that finding a way to manage strong emotions is imperative to all of us.

When grieving, dealing with the raw and troublesome personal truths surrounding losses can be one of the most difficult things to face. The pain of looking candidly at things we might have done wrong, forgotten to do, or overlooked can feel so excruciating that it feels as if it might destroy us. We would rather do almost anything than look directly at this. However, without proper perspective, remorse can become the seed of a kind of chronic guilt that can stay with us much longer than our mourning.

Methods for staying with these fallible parts of ourselves can be immensely helpful in order not to intensify our suffering by falling into the trap of self-denigration and violence.

The antidote to this aspect of grief involves practices that remind us of our basic goodness.

The sixth gift of grief is that it gives us direct access to the deep well of peace and stillness around and inside us, which offers us the opportunity to practice managing strong emotions. One path to this freedom is to access stillness in the midst of turbulent feelings. For me, stillness contemplation remains one of the most calming exercises when I am in the midst of strong, overwhelming emotion. Underneath all of the commotion, it is such a relief to access a kind of peace at the center of things, and to know that it is constant, always there for us, just waiting to be noticed, no matter what level of suffering we encounter. Connecting with the stillness around and inside of us puts things in perspective. We are reminded that we are not our suffering: we do not consist only of our regrets. When we turn this peace, or gentleness, toward ourselves, we experience forgiveness, for our mistakes, for our misjudgments, and for our simple humanness.

* * *

ANTIDOTE TO GRIEF
6. Stillness Contemplation:
An antidote to remorse

STILLNESS CONTEMPLATION

Become aware of the stillness underneath all movement. Movement is ripples on the surface of life itself. Imagine a deep ocean. You are the ocean. Your thoughts are like waves on the surface of the ocean. Sometimes they are big; at its worst, life may feel like a hurricane or a tsunami- the waves may even feel like they are drowning us. Sometimes the ocean is calm and reflects everything around it like a mirror- it holds everything in itself momentarily.

Underneath the waves a vast deep well of still water always exists. This is who you really are, and you can access it at any time. The ocean's surface is a minute percentage of its real depth- the largest wave at the top may be 100 feet, but the depth and stillness of the ocean goes down for thousands of feet- it drops off the continental shelf and goes down for miles. No one really knows how deep it goes- it is immeasurable.

Keep your attention on the motionless part of the ocean, on the still point at the very center of your being- silent, spacious, tranquil. Let your attention emanate from this point to encompass every part of your being. Feel your remorse as waves on the surface of a deep ocean of placidity inside you- a vast gentle well of peace. This stillness is always accessible to you. Anytime you feel caught up in waves of emotions, thoughts, or physical discomfort, you can dive into the gentle waters of kindness, and the limitless stillness below.

7

CONNECTION

Riveted
It is possible that things will not get better
than they are now, or have been known to be.
It is possible that we are past the middle now.
It is possible that we have crossed the great water
without knowing it, and stand now on the other side.
Yes: I think we have crossed it. Now
we are being given tickets, and they are not
tickets to the show we had been thinking of,
but to a different show, clearly inferior.
Check again: it is our own name on the envelope.
The tickets are to that other show.
It is possible that we will walk out of the darkened hall
without waiting for the last act: people do.
Some people do. But it is probable
that we will stay seated in our narrow seats
all through the tedious dénouement
to the unsurprising end - riveted, as it were;
spellbound by our own imperfect lives
because they are lives,
and because they are ours.
~Robyn Sarah

~

...Through the bow window, you are now beset with a grim image of the woman, out of bed after many days with little food, facing the harsh flourescent lights in a superstore. You have a hard time recognizing her as the same person you saw in her memories- so rich and bountiful and she so happy. Because of her expression, her face appears completely different, sunken and discolored. She is attempting to fill out a check but it appears that she is unable to write, her hand is so shaky, and then you see her giving up and somehow trying to fish out her credit card to pay for a small package of bullets. Who is waiting on her? Are they paying any attention? You know what this is leading to now, and it makes you wonder, how many times you have had some chance or barely human exchange with someone on their way to killing themselves without even knowing it...

THE STORY

Back on the big red couches in the Hunt Memorial Library, as we are every few weeks, we proceed on this voyage together. We are all wrecked emotionally- in the throws of major grief and shock. We are miserable, and for the first time in our lives none of us is denying it. This feels somehow freeing- that we could have this kind of emotional connection as a family. It is completely new to us: a kind of openhearted relationship with pain that is not our natural instinct.

We receive the results of the autopsy that was performed. We were hoping, counting even, on some kind of terrible diagnosis- ALS, or Alzheimer's, something more significant that she could have been running from than just us and our family. We are disheartened to find out that she was a perfectly healthy, sixty four year old woman. *So, it was just the bogie-man that got her,* my father muses.

From the police, we learn that she purchased the gun from the local pawnshop nine days before her death. We all trace the timeline back, trying to work out what was happening. She had already visited Dr. F twice. She was on her third medication. She had been in this black state of depression for only 6 weeks. Couldn't she have held on any longer? Words from a graduate course in psychology float across my awareness; *every crisis resolves itself in one way or another in 4-6 weeks.*

We look through my mother's belongings for more clues. We find a check still in her checkbook, with four letters of her name written out by a shaky hand in the signature line B-A-R-B and the date 10/19/04. The check was never fully made out. What was she trying to pay for by check- the bullets, the gun, something else?

The painful reality that she planned this: that she lied to me on numerous occasions when I asked her about suicide;

that she could barely get out of bed but seemed to be able to drive the fifteen minutes to the pawn shop for the gun and then to Wal-Mart to get the bullets for it; that she planned it for when my father would be out, double checking the night before and then waiting for him to leave for his dentist appointment that morning; this relentlessly secret life she led up until the end is all encompassing, and brings a pain almost too difficult to bear.

When I asked her about suicide, she responded as if the thought had never occurred to her, as if she hadn't the strength to consider any such thing. Maybe she lied out of fear of being hospitalized. Maybe she lied to maintain the option, the sense of control that such a plan would bring. Maybe she had been on medication just long enough to give her the strength to get out of bed and drive herself to buy the gun, and just long enough to be able to walk to the end of the dock.

There is no way to answer these questions, and yet I cannot stop asking them. I do know that she had little strength to get out of bed- to do anything but feel dizzy and cry, to eat or drink. In light of all of this I still cannot understand how she had the strength to bring about further self-destruction.

We are trying to solve a mystery, and we cling alternately to the belief that things will be better if we can make some sense of this and to the knowledge that ultimately we can never know what really happened and that there is little that can soften the stark truth of her brutal death. Are we thinking we can change the ending somehow? This may be a futile journey, yet we feel we have no choice but to walk it. So far, we have discovered no great answers except the immensity of what can be found in love, comfort, and holding together to face things full in the face, a task that would certainly be impossible alone.

With Dr. F, we re-explore the loss of our estranged youngest sister, who had chosen to divorce herself from the family ten years before. For my mother, it was devastating. It had sat like an open wound- a central source of unresolved pain and a repository for much of her deep misery. Stored in her bedside drawer, which she slept next to every night, was every piece of fraught communication that passed between them over the past 10 years. Unfortunately, her anguish about this loss never came hand in hand with any kind of peace about it.

Our sister's abrupt, aggressive withdrawal from the family was our first abandonment, exacerbated because the reasons for it had never been fully understood or explained. It was a pain we all shared, but which caused unique tension for each of us. Opening this old wound and looking at our mutual sense of rejection at this point is deeply painful, but it brings a kind of closure for us that I wish my mother could have experienced with regard to her youngest daughter.

With my fathers and remaining sisters, it is a wonderful solace to simply experience the comfort of being together in this foreign world that only we understand. We talk. We walk the labyrinth. We offer silence. My father cooks us a nice hot meal. We sleep, knit, lie on the couches and laugh with a kind of twisted sense of what is funny that only the four of us can understand.

We joke about being dumped and abandoned in such a direct way, not once, but by two members of the family. We laugh about the ridiculous gruesomeness of our visit to the undertaker. We joke about aspects of the service and the minister, about Dr. F., and the casserole women, kidding about them offering a certain kind of comfort with the food. We try to resurrect my mother's funny spot-on observations about humanity in its various forms. As we walk through the heart of darkness, the consolation our sense of togetherness provides is vital to us all.

With my mother's suicide, there is a release from the energetic ties that had held us all in place for so long, unable to move forward. There were ways in which I was bound with her, and unconsciously held myself back so that she could stay where she was, and so we remained a bit frozen in life, afraid to move forward. I think we all felt a release from some kind of constriction that we had never even known existed in our family. The web was broken and it felt both painful and freeing at the same time.

We had gotten so used to interacting in certain familiar ways, to falling into old roles, that they became static and we had begun to see each other as flat two-dimensional beings, less than human. Now we were liberated from that. As shock slowly wore off, we were all left so raw and uncomfortable that we were more open to one another.

It is said that when one parent dies, we lose both for a while. The surviving parent is lost to grief. An unusual gift of my mother's suicide was that I actually gained a part of my father I did not really have access to before. He had come out from the shadow of my mother and I was seeing parts of him for the first time. I don't know whether they had been there all along or whether I was just noticing them. I was left amazed and inspired by his honesty in looking at the past and by his bravery to continue walk this difficult path.

I experienced a new connection with my sisters as well. While Miranda and I had always been emotionally close and often seemed to see things in a similar light, our family culture was not one of direct expressions of caring and love. Miranda and I began to back up our emotional closeness with heartfelt expressions to one another, which were a balm during times of doubt.

As for my older sister, a part of me had always been somewhat intimidated by Julia. Being the oldest, she had been the one to chase in our family. By nature, or at least in the family dynamic, she was not someone who talked easily and openly about feelings and emotions. This changed in family therapy however. It was Julia who helped me to see my mother in a more sympathetic light. Somehow, while I had just been annoyed with my mother's depression over the summer, Julia was able to convey and help me relate to the raw pain underneath her stupor.

I knew that all this was only possible because of my mother's suicide. Without it, we would not be relating to one another in such a deep and supportive way. This confused me, because while I felt grateful for these gifts I did not want to feel grateful for such a horrible thing happening in our family. Dr. F clarified this tumult in such a beautiful way: *What she did is not the reason for the gifts you are experiencing as a result of it. There is no gift in the final act. The gift comes from your choices in the face of it.*

Every visit, I sit in the corner of the boathouse at the end of the dock, trying to imagine what she was experiencing as she sat there in her last moments. I watch the light play on the surface of the water. I wonder where the rest of the bullets are. I look for hidden bloodstains, parts of her I may have missed. Would I find the box of bullets if I dove underneath the water? I marvel at how beautiful the last images she saw and heard were- the giant trees on the horizon, the sounds of silence, the ceaseless movement of the water- and I wonder at how disconnected she must have been from them, and how she could have become so disconnected from us all.

The DSM V, the diagnostic manual for psychological syndromes and disorders, defines complex grief as including the hallmark symptoms of confusion about life's role, diminished sense of self, and a feeling that life is empty or meaningless. Perhaps that was why we as a family clung so hard to one another during our initial grieving. We needed to feel that there was still some kind of meaning. I felt detached from everything else. I still felt great love for and a deep attachment to my husband and son, but I also know that because of my internal journey, there was a part of me that was unavailable to them during this period.

Despite my disconnection, my husband was, from the beginning, silent supportive, and steadfast- a lesson in grace. I noticed this like a soft pillow onto which I constantly fell back, grateful and exhausted. Though I could not always express it (the thought of trying to do anything other than carry the load of grief felt so exhausting), I was constantly aware of and knew that I could not have survived without the loving silence he held for me. The quiet, protective space with which he surrounded me, and this foundation of love underneath it, was the greatest gift he could ever have given. He cupped my heart and held it gently in peace, and gave me a reminder of the best in humanity during a time when I had been exposed to the worst of it.

* * *

A GREATER PERSPECTIVE

As my grief progressed from shock, there were so many questions crowding in on my mind, I found it extremely helpful to focus on the silence underneath the thoughts. I could find it by remembering the day of my mother's funeral, when we were all out on the water. It helped me put into perspective all of my jumbled thoughts, including this burning desire to understand, which were at their base just energetic move-ments, or "noise", that moved and changed in each passing moment. The practice of silence helped me to bear witness to the thoughts rather than pushing them down or away so they built up and re-emerged at a later time, stronger and more muddied up in some other emotional storm. The silent field of stillness was always there, gently muffling the noise of my thought and emotions.

The silence gave me access to **the seventh gift of grief, an instant deepened connection with loved ones that oc-curs during great loss, which can help heal old emotional wounds.** This profound deepening of bonds occurs in the af-termath of death. There is an energy of love surrounding us as we grieve, held there by those who deeply care for us and the ones we have lost. In this way, we are fortunate to have others with whom to journey, who can demonstrate and remind us of the deep love inherent in humanity. In silence, we can access this tenderness, which acts as a balm for the pain of the deep emotional anguish that accompanies loss. With a background of silence, we can feel the deep abounding love surrounding us, and this connection puts the ache of our loss and previous losses on our lives into a greater perspective.

* * *

ANTIDOTE TO GRIEF
7. Silence contemplation:
An antidote to stark emotional anguish

SILENCE CONTEMPLATION

In the attitude of silence the soul finds the path in a clearer light, and what is elusive and deceptive resolves itself into crystal clearness. ~Mahatma Gandhi

Listen for the silence in which all sound happens. Every sound is born out of silence, dies, and retreats back into the peace from which it came. Nature governs itself in this perfect quiet. Become aware of the silence in which sounds happen. Notice the hush between breaths, between sounds, into which a sound retreats. Like the calm quiet of a newly fallen snow, allow silence to blanket the noise of this moment. Expand your awareness of this already present feature of each moment. In silence, we can find a connection to others that is much deeper than language. We can also make space for feelings and unresolved pain. Allow the silent field of stillness to envelop your pain in quiet awareness.

Practice silence for a period of time each day- a half-hour, or each week (for example, Sunday morning from 8-10am will be spent in quiet). It will make you aware of how many wasted words we all use; how much unnecessary noise we make.

8

THE MYSTERY OF BIRTH AND DEATH

*We think that the point is to pass the test or to overcome the problem, but the truth is
that things don't really get solved. They come together and they fall apart. Then they come
together and fall apart again. It's just like that. The healing comes from letting there be room
for all of this to happen: room for grief, for relief, for misery, for joy.*
~ Pema Chodron

THE STORY

The indefatigable way in which we as a family approached our grieving was definitely out of character for us. I
am sure a part of it was that we all knew somehow that my
mother's death had been caused by a life of unprocessed emotions, a life of running from pain, and that we wanted the antidote for it. If the remedy for suicide was the dogged inspection
of even the worst imaginable pain, then we were in. For a
while this investigation phase consumed us- this cycle of being
mystified and disappointed, alternately fascinated and appalled
by what had happened.

Another part of it was that we needed to find some relief
from the extreme discomfort of the reality that we had not
been able to save her. Suicide meant that my mother had made
a choice to leave, and to be with the stark fact that she would
rather not be on earth than be here with us was not easy. After
having been abandoned in this complete way, we were walking
a gauntlet of confusing emotions. The most obvious one was
guilt. Rarely in any other form of death do people encounter
such a direct sense of responsibility. The major burden for us
was that we might have done something, anything, to have
prevented this drastic outcome.

Added to all of this I also felt overwhelmed by the violence of my mother's death. It seemed like the ultimate act of

anger. I could not connect with this level of vehemence and brutality. Shooting was the most violent thing I could imagine doing. When I pictured myself in that kill or be killed scenario, for me it was never much of a dilemma- be killed. I would rather die than live with having taken a human life, whatever the circumstances. But to commit the murder of yourself? And in such an explosive way? This seemed incomprehensible to me, and yet I could not help trying to wrap my mind around it over and over as I grieved. The desperate need to understand and the inner knowledge of the unfathomability of the act went hand in hand in our grieving process.

Her death was a crime, and as with any crime I found myself going over the details in my mind, looking for clues. Which version was right? Calculating, calm, logical killer; haunted specter with one earplug, barely able to walk; angry, hysterical abandoned psychotic with a big explosive ending- the ultimate act of anger; or pathetic, tortured soul barely able to pull the trigger?

The deep suffering that could have led to this, and that she kept it all so well hidden, continued to be unbearably painful to me. I would picture her, as I always did, crouching in the boathouse, gun in her mouth, in her final moments. When I fell into this deep suffering, I imagined myself in her body just as she shot herself- I could feel the cold metal push back a bit too far and high in my throat, higher than I would have expected; felt the explosion not that painful; the wound in the back of my head; the metallic taste of blood. There was an odd kind of comfort to be found in fantasizing that I could feel what she felt.

In bed at night, I found myself talking to her, trying to find answers:

Mom, why were your eyes open when Dad found you? I just pic-
tured them closed, like you would need to screw up all of your strength.
Miranda says your eyes were open because you were determined to get it
right- the angle of the gun, the direction it was pointing. You wanted to see
it to make sure you had it correctly positioned. Maybe your eyes flew open
as a side effect of the jarring to your head. Your poor head.

We process our anger at the doctor- the one who saw her
the first time for twenty minutes, prescribed her Prozac, never
returned her phone calls or asked to see her when she reported
disturbing symptoms, and changed her prescription to Lexiprau through the nurse *without ever having seen her again.* How
could he not have even called her back? But then it is entirely
possible my mother never let on just how much discomfort
she was in.

We want to hate the man in the pawnshop who sold her
the gun, but upon visiting there and talking to him, I find that
he is so kind that I cannot. He shows us the gun (I get the
strong sense that it is the actual gun, but I think he wants to
spare us this information) and tells us of his conversation with
my mother.

I continue to be spellbound by the books she left by her
bed. What was meant by them? She had been unable to read
the last four weeks. She had been drunk the last night. Why
had she left a book *on the bed,* on top of the covers she had just
gotten out from under? Home Before Dark is a memoir by a
daughter about her alcoholic father, but the thing is, he recov-
ers and gets better and goes on to lead a totally successful life.
So her leaving this book feels like some kind of cruel joke. Or
maybe she was reaching for a successful ending up until her
last moments?

And her favorite children's book, Through the Mickle
Woods, is about a man's journey through grief. It feels like a

complete minimalization to my father, as if she was saying; *don't worry, you'll move on.* As if she was trying to excuse herself for the inexcusable thing she was about to do. And then, if these even were messages, I realize that whatever she was saying from her dark world must have been completely insane. Still, I can't help but be caught up in the mystery of which mother left those books and what she wanted to say to us in her last moments of life.

Here is another question: Why the one earplug in her ear? She slept with them in most nights. Did she forget to take it out? Did she leave it in on purpose to protect herself from hearing the sound of the gun? Such an absurdly self-caretaking gesture. Like the coat she wore. Why wear a coat, or shoes? Why care if you were going to be cold? It is senseless to ponder these incongruities, and illogical to try and put myself in a psychotic suicidal person's head. Despite knowing this, my mind keeps trying to fit this unnatural event into the natural order of the world.

* * *

A GREATER PERSPECTIVE

Separating thoughts from feelings was helpful to me during the grieving process, and even more helpful was being able to distinguish between the actual pain I experienced and the suffering thoughts I created (which intensified the pain more). Pain is what we experience. Suffering is what our mind makes of that experience. Suffering is created by thoughts.

I could see that when I spent too long asking unanswerable questions or imagining I could read my mother's mind, it made the pain worse. Getting stuck in the why's felt like it would never lead to relief, and I found the practice of separating my own thoughts from the rest of my experience extremely helpful.

My goal was to feel the actual pain of the event and the grief without unnecessarily expanding it or getting stuck in it. I know that in my own case, there was a part of me that thought that if I figured out why this had happened, it would somehow soften the pain of it. However, my puzzling just led to more suffering, because there was no certain answer. Death, in whatever way it comes, is a mystery that the mind cannot comprehend. So the more we can separate our thoughts about the event from the actual event, the more smoothly we can move through the unanswerable aspects of death.

The **eighth gift of grief, then, is that is puts us in touch with the mystery of death.** This opportunity to be with the mysterious process that we will all go through is the closest thing we will get to having a blueprint for it.

Death is a lot like birth: an enigmatic process guided by the greater wisdom of the body. Most of us can never imagine wanting to die, but in people who are actively dying we can witness an increasing "onward absorption" that moves them away from incarnation. Similarly, at birth, the infant body carries a kind of dedicated attention, an inner knowing that, along with the intelligence of the mother's body, guides and positions it through and out of the birth canal.

In order to know what it is like to be born, we must rely on some kind of inherent wisdom, a remembrance of our own experience, imprinted somewhere in our subconscious, an obscure place where we store all of the collective memories of our life thus far. In order to know death, we must rely on some kind of internal connection to a collective human consciousness that lies beyond our intellectualization of the event.

The closest we can come to this inner knowing is through our own experiences with death, loss, and grieving.

* * *

ANTIDOTE TO GRIEF
8. Open Sky Contemplation:
An antidote to intellectualization

OPEN SKY CONTEMPLATION

Picture a vast blue sky. Imagine that you are the sky. Now imagine that your thoughts are clouds. Each cloud represents a feeling or a thought. Watch the clouds, the speed at which they move, their density. At times the sky might be totally clear. Other times it may be full of clouds, all strung together with no space in between like one long white haze. Some clouds may be fluffy and white, and some may be dense and dark and full of rain. Just watch the clouds as they roll by. Watch their cycle of life and death, how they appear and disappear. Each cloud comes into existence, moves and shifts for a while, and then goes out of existence. Now allow yourself to focus on the blue sky underneath the clouds, bright with the light of the sun. You are the blue sky, and remain constant throughout all of the movement of the various thoughts and emotions. You are the greater awareness in which the thoughts happen. You are the constant in a constantly changing skyscape.

9

THE FLOW OF LIFE

In a dark time the eye begins to see.
~ Theodore Roethke

THE STORY

In this period of trying to fit the suicide into an explainable occurrence, alcohol and the role it played in her demise was difficult to see clearly. It was a lifelong battle she had fought and it had been a part of our family story from the beginning. For a while I thought it bore the bulk of responsibility. I blamed her for choosing it and for self-destructing with it. Then I blamed it: the disease. It was her ultimate shadow struggle, one that went back many generations, with which she had many ups and downs, and one she could never completely conquer. Did she feel this failure at the end?

A few weeks after her death, my father was cleaning out my mother's Jeep. He found a plastic bag with a receipt for three bottles of liquor dated a month before her death. He had already found a receipt for four bottles of liquor dated from five weeks before. The bottles were nowhere to be found, but that isn't unusual since for an alcoholic, hiding bottles can be an art. But despite the many years of living with this disease, just how much she may really have been drinking and how much all of this was a major part of her demise stunned us all.

Just what was the real extent of her drinking at the end? How could my father, who lived with her, not have seen this? We all thought, as she told us, that it was this major depressive breakdown of unknown source with troubling neurological symptoms- tremors, blackouts, and slurring.

Alcohol was a part of her equation, but I had thought she was basically incapable of drinking extensively because she was so unbelievably depressed. Throughout her life, she had been an up and down alcoholic, with periods that included heavy, moderate, light, and no drinking. Over the summer, she had been drinking and using over the counter sleeping pills, but this was "normal" in terms of her behavior on and off over the years.

I took most of her symptoms to be from depression. Now it occurred to me suddenly that they could just as easily be from an advanced alcoholic binge- no appetite, tired all day, sleeping (from staying up all night drinking), blackouts, vomiting, tremors, shaking, slurring, slow talking. What a mess she was. What an extra secret she was keeping. *Why isn't anyone helping me!?!* she had cried to me. *I don't know how much longer I can hang on. Why isn't the medicine working?* Was she drinking during the day? How long, how much? Was the alcohol nullifying the effect of the medication? It felt like such a betrayal. She had chosen alcohol over the people in her life time and time again throughout her life, and she now had chosen to die and keep alcohol rather than live and stay with us and risk having to be found out, to have to give it up and get better.

That alcohol bore a great responsibility I saw- the suicide would not have happened without it- but I also recognized that that was only one side of her multi-layered story. Looking at it through that model alone really narrowed her life down to only one dimension of it. I was beginning to realize that I could make a lot of explanations fit, but never perfectly. For example, I found this book of a review of Prozac containing chapters full of examples of people who had gone on Prozac, even low doses (the book mentions 20mgs- similar to her dose) and then had sudden inexplicable violent psychosis resulting in suicide. It listed person after person, some committing suicide within two weeks of taking the drug. They had no history of depression, suicide attempts, nothing. They suddenly just left the eggs frying in the pan and walked in another room and hung or shot themselves.

Survivors of these experiences recount the horrifying monsters in their head: an unbelievable hell. They have never experienced anything like it before or since. In fact, there is a whole national network of support for Prozac survivors and the families left behind- either they survived taking the drug or they have survived a family member's suicide from the drug.[4] Isn't the side effect of suicidal thoughts one of the warnings on a Prozac bottle?

This profile fit my mother as well. Her behavior and decline was sudden, rapid, and occurred within a week of beginning Prozac. She could not get out of bed- everything became black- she said she would lay in bed and try not to think. She had blackouts, would fall down, throw up, could not eat. Then I think, if I were experiencing this kind of hell, and alcohol was my one form of emotional support, wouldn't I look to it for relief? Of course. Who could not have compassion for this attempt at alleviation in the face of such a large devil, even though it may have helped cause and precipitate her downfall and exacerbated the bad effects of these carelessly prescribed drugs.

So I see that alcohol and this medication played some role in her death as well. It was so many things. Her coping mechanisms- alcoholism, extreme emotional repression, running away, and perhaps an innate vulnerable quality inside her all configured in some perfect storm that culminated in that awful morning.

We had tried blaming everything: ourselves, our youngest sister, alcohol, Prozac, the doctor who failed to monitor the

Prozac or her symptoms, the Virginia no-wait for firearm purchase law, the man in the pawn shop who sold her the gun, the superstore that sold the bullets. I was exhausted, because no one explanation seemed to fit right. It was a bizarre configuration of a person's life gone awry and everything and nothing was responsible. Like the full moon eclipse on the night she died, it was a web of factors so complex that I would never be able to unravel them or completely understand.

We were better off getting comfortable with the mystery of it, and with the extreme juxtapositions of life itself.

* * *

A GREATER PERSPECTIVE

My intense need to find some kind of explanation for my mother's death was an example of one of the seven stages of grief: bargaining. Bargaining results from a desire to lessen the pain of mourning. It is an intellectual effort to control our suffering. In my own case, I wanted to make sense of my mother's unaccountable act, and I thought that if I could comprehend it, I could somehow lessen the painful effect of it. Part of this need to explain was also that on some unconscious level, I thought that if I handled my mother's death well, there would be some kind of reward for me at the end. I was bargaining with life, trying to arrange the outcome of my experience because I could not assimilate the pain of it.

I found that running beneath this was a fundamental perception that there is no way to comprehend everything about this life, and that there are some mysteries we will never solve. We do not need to decipher nor explain everything. The more we can go with the flow of the different things that life throws our way, the less we need to understand, and the more smoothly we can move through any difficult or unexplainable experience.

In times when there are no answers, acceding to life's greater flow can be extremely comforting. The perpetual movement of life itself is a constant into which we can fall back when our mind is unable to explain death's mysteries.

The ninth gift of grief is that it offers us the opportunity to give way to the rhythm of life. In this flow, we can let go of the need to control and explain all aspects of our experience. We have a forum to begin to absorb life's unanswerable questions.

* * *

ANTIDOTE TO GRIEF
9. Flow of Life Meditation:
An antidote to control

FLOW OF LIFE CONTEMPLATION

Get in touch with life's flow like a river moving in and around everything. You are the river. You are the fast moving water, bubbling and rushing over the rocks it encounters, eddying and swirling in one place for a time and then moving with the current. As the water, you do not become stuck in any one area, trying to fathom the depths or natural movements of the flow. You keep moving with the current.

Notice the direction of the flow- and let your attention follow it. Let life's greater direction be your orientation. Follow the current with your attention. Sometimes the water is moving very fast and sometimes it is almost still. Notice the difference between flowing with the current of life and fighting against it. Life is in perpetual motion, but your attention is the constant. Allow your attention to move with the current of life as it changes and shifts with each moment. Now expand your awareness to include the shore as well. You are the ground, the awareness, which holds the moving water and absorbs this constant change into your being.

Your awareness is the container that can hold the water, the ground, and the movement of both all at once. As you go through your day, keep some of your attention on noticing the current in which life is directing you. Allow yourself to be carried by the flow of life, and notice if this cooperation expands your sense of ease and greater symmetry.

10

GREATER FORCES AT WORK

People like us, who believe in physics, know that the distinction between past, present, and future is only a stubbornly persistent illusion.
~ Albert Einstein

THE STORY

From the moment she died, I experienced a number of dreams, synchronicities, and experiences of serendipity that continued to remind me that life was bigger and more intelligent than I was. Call it faith, spirit, or God, continuing to let go into that was a great comfort. It had begun with the heron the night of her death. It kept us company all that night, squawking and flying back and forth along the shore as we sat in the full moon at the end of the dock. To my sisters and me it just seemed so clear that this heron was directly connected to her, or somehow *was* her. Many months later, my father hired a sculptor to create a memorial plaque for her, and the artist was directed to come up with some sketches of something simple and natural- whatever struck him. The sculptor sent back a sketch of a heron flying under a full moon. We were astonished. Neither my father nor the sculptor had known anything of our experience with the heron and the moon on the night of my mother's death.

We are inextricably linked to our mothers whether they are physically present or not. The idea of mother is so ingrained in our psyche that whether we are close in distance or not, our mother feels a deep part of us. For a time, she was with us on this journey- she was an integral part, her spirit seemingly hovering around us. Whether she was close to us in actuality, or whether it was just that she was such a deep part of our psyche that she seemed close, I am unsure, but regardless, she appeared to us during that time in numerous dreams, visions and memories, and I would always awake from them feeling like I had really encountered her.

One particularly powerful one was where I found myself visiting her in a mental hospital situated in the clouds. She was in a kind of hospital gown and we met in a visitors area that looked like an old fashioned kitchen, with a formica table and metal-legged chairs. Her parents were her guards and had brought her out from another part of the ward. She looked weak and shaky. She was crying and said it was very hard. *Is it hard for you that they are here?*, I asked her, referring to her parents. *No, they are helping me. I have to stay here for a while. I have to look at some things and they can help me. I'll be here about six weeks and then I can move on.*

Another time I had a dream that was more than a dream, where she appeared on my bed, laying across from me. This felt so palpably real to me I still find it difficult to believe it could have only been my unconscious. I was ecstatic to see her, and I immediately began talking to her. It quickly became clear that she would only remain so intensely clear to me if I could just accept her appearance, and not ask questions. I could not help myself and began peppering her with questions, but as I asked, she began to disintegrate, and soon disappeared entirely.

I experienced a strong and frequent desire to process the details of what was happening to me with my mother- I constantly wanted to call her, often thinking of how she would react to something annoying or funny that happened during the whole process of her death and its aftermath. I wanted to share my feelings about this momentous life event with her. A lot of my dreams had to do with her showing up and me so eager to process the event of her death with her.

Though the details were different, the main theme of the dreams was always the same. In it my sisters, father and I were on our path together; processing what happened, mourning together, holding each other up. And suddenly, my mother would show up in the room, or at the dinner table, or in the closet where we were sorting through her things. She had killed herself but now she was back. I would be so stunned, but so excited like a child on Christmas Day who was getting the best surprise I could think of. This was the reward for all of my good behavior, for all of the hard work we had been doing as a family.

Mom!, I would exclaim, *you're back!* She would smile and agree. I was so happy to see her. We all were. We would bask in the pleasure of her amazing return. I would ask her all kinds of questions about what it was like on the other side and how she got back. Some questions she could answer and others she said she wasn't allowed to tell. And in some dreams, if I pressed too hard about why she had done it, she would become upset and start to disappear again. So I learned to follow the rules. Just be happy she was here now. Don't ask too many questions. Don't try to figure it out.

And then there would come the point in the dream when I realized that her return was absurd in the eyes of the real world. How were we going to explain it to everyone? They would be so shocked, and how would they understand? It was unusual enough to choose death that way, but then to come back from the dead! So the vision continued with our family in a secret world only we could understand. We had lost something and then it had come back to us. We all understood that now.

After awhile, when my mother showed up in my dreams, I didn't want her to be back. She was the same person as when she left, and we had all become so different. We had been forced to by what she had done. How could she fit in to our family anymore? We had all worked so hard to understand her death, to fit it into our lives, to move forward from the pool of grief she had left behind. And she was stuck in time; the mother who had abandoned us- who had chosen to go. She was the one who had caused all of this; who had taken a gun to her head one pretty fall morning- murderer and victim at the same time. How could she have done such a thing? She had a lot to answer for, not just about life on the other side, but also about why she had put us through all of this in the first place.

Consciously, I realized I could not control what she did by having her explain it. Or by coming up with my own perfect explanation of what happened and why it did. What was the use? Would it bring her back? Ultimately, this is unknowable. We think that if we can understand these things that it will somehow soften the pain of it. We even magically believe that we can make things go away, or make a person return from the dead. We bargain with the truth in our minds, as if we could change the stark reality of something that has already happened.

* * *

A GREATER PERSPECTIVE

Visitations, dreams, and numinous occurrences are extremely common to grievers. These experiences can provide relief by introducing or deepening a faith in a force greater than ourselves. The serendipity we feel is evidence of some greater design. We become aware of the many unseen forces at work in the universe.

My recurring dreams were another example of the bargaining that accompanies mourning. The nature of them revealed that there was an unconscious part of me that truly believed that if I followed certain rules, my mother might be returned to me. This may also have been a desire to have life as I knew it before returned to me just at the same time that I was beginning to let go of my old story.

The many synchronicities that occur when we grieve help to ease the intensity of the loss we have just experienced. They also strengthen our connection to the greater mystery that is death. We sense that even though the person is no longer in physical form, they are still surrounding us. It may well be no accident that this sense is strongest in the moments most closely following a loved one's death, when our multi-sensory perception is heightened. In this way again, death resembles birth. The nearer to its birth a baby is, the more precious the energy it emits to those around it. It is much the same with returning from whence we came.

Letting go into something larger than myself was easier for me during my intense grieving because, try as I might, there was no way my mind could make sense of the world, as it had just fallen apart so completely for me. Trusting in a greater power provided great consolation to me. Surrendering to forces beyond our understanding can ease the tension that accompanies the chasm that is left when someone we love leaves this life.

The tenth gift of grief is that it exposes us to impressions of forces greater than ourselves at work in the universe. Experiences of these unseen forces can bring solace to the immediate experience of missing our loved one and the craving for their impossible return. They can also provide relief in the face of our immediate sense of loss. No matter what our individual spiritual beliefs, surrender contemplation can help us to connect with and be open to the larger mysteries of the soul, the body, life and its energies.

ANTIDOTE TO GRIEF
10. Surrender contemplation:
An antidote to bargaining

SURRENDER CONTEMPLATION:
A GREATER INTELLIGENCE

Feel the sensations in the inner body. Perceive the greater intelligence at work in the body. Sense your breath. Allow yourself to feel the connection between it and the greater forces at work in nature and beyond. Let you awareness expand to the farthest reaches of the universe- to the most distant star in the galaxy and then into galaxies beyond this one. These larger forces persist despite your lack of understanding of or attention to them. Notice yourself as part of this greater design.

Be aware of the energetic light connection between your body, your breath, space, planets, and galaxies. Surrender to this great interconnectivity of life, beyond your limited understanding but so intelligent, so immense it is incalculable. Allow this mystery to experience itself through you. Let life do the work. Lift up your arms to the sky, in homage to this greater force at work in all life.

11

ALIVENESS

Mourning, the act of dealing with grief, requires attention.
~Joan Dideon

THE STORY

Grieving a suicide comes with its own unique complexities, and, therefore, its own traps in which to get stuck along the way. Many people never move beyond it. It ruins lives, and family members and loved ones are the main victims, because they are the ones left to deal with the psychological wreckage left behind by this act.

Suicide is, quite literally, self-murder. Therefore, survivors have the uncommon upset of being family to a victim of murder. At the same time, we have the shame of being family members of a killer, compiled with our anger at that criminal. In the final trifecta of sorrow, we carry the ultimate humiliation of the fact that the person the murderer chose to slaughter was herself.

It is hard to come to terms with the fact that your own mother is a murderer, and that the person she chose to slay was your mother. Bizarrely, I felt shame and humiliation that my mother was a killer, took it personally that she had killed my mother, while feeling anguish that my mother had been the victim of a murder.

Suicide is aberrant: it upsets the natural order. In the case of my mother, it provided a contrast that was difficult for me to fathom. That she, who had such a visceral response to beauty, could have chosen to do it in the midst of such natural harmony was agitating. She was a person who woke up to capture an incredible sunrise, who would cry over a beautiful piece of china. How could she have become so unmoved by life? I felt so disconnected from the choice she made that for a long time I couldn't find any happy memories of her. I was so busy trying to find the hidden darkness that had caused this that I lost the magical parts of who she had been.

Another factor to deal with in suicide is a sense of abandonment, which is compounded when it is by a parent. In the case of my mother, my lifegiver had taken her own. Just as with any particular experience of grief, no one who has not experienced suicide can really understand this fully. It just cannot be known. A mother, the most primal relationship, chose to leave. Even at thirty-nine, this felt like the ultimate abandonment.

There is also an obvious sense of responsibility. We all felt that there must have been a chance, just one possibility that we could have changed something and kept her alive, and that potential existed up until the moment she died. That is why we had to trace every step. We wanted to find out when that moment could have been. Survivors have to become comfortable with this truth, and with the ultimate question, *did we allow her to die?*

Though it is not a popular emotion, anger was a very useful one to my family. It told us that our old life was gone. We were being re-born to a new one, and any resistance hurt and slowed down the rebirthing process. Sometimes, anger was the fuel that we used to propel us forward when we did not think we could take another step.

My personal anger came in several forms. First, while I did not feel a resistance to or denial about the suicide itself, I often felt angry about the changes forced upon me by it. It felt like my life had completely fallen apart because of someone else's willful act. I also experienced the anger as a fire that helped me keep going in the face of enormous pain. In addition, being angry at my mother created a separation with her that allowed me to begin to let her go.

One of the common characteristics of people who commit suicide is a chronic need for control. The victim chooses the timing and manner of their own death. Paradoxically, the thing that my mother was trying to achieve by her suicide- a sense of control- resulted in my complete loss of it. I felt a sense of helplessness and an absolute loss of control about the world around me. I had tumbled through the horizon into this new country, and I now recognized that things as I knew them could totally fall to pieces at any moment, and I was subject to it all, fully vulnerable.

Because of this need for control, assessing suicide risk is a complex and uncertain process. The possible victim is in complete command of how much she chooses to share with a therapist or family member. My mother had been very secretive about what she was planning because she wanted to preserve her right to carry out her intentions without interference. This was no cry for help. To tell someone what she was considering would mean to give up dominion over the only escape she could devise from her nightmare and would leave her facing what was in her eyes an even more nightmarish scenario: hospitalization. Psychiatric hospitals often increase suicide risk: they have a completed suicide rate almost 35% greater than in the community.[5]

I struggled enormously with not having identified my mother's imminent risk. I knew things were coming to a head for her, but I had assessed her at a moderate to low risk for suicide. I knew that in her case, hospitalization would increase her symptoms of depression and breakdown, because it would force her to face her worst fear at a time when she already felt helpless, out of control, and petrified. It took me a long while to become comfortable with the fact that I just couldn't see the situation clearly.

The American Psychological Association identifies eleven critical risk factors in assessing suicide [6], and it frustrated my attempts to understand things that my mother met only the final three of these. She had no previous suicide attempts, had expressed no previous attraction to death, had no family history of suicide, she was not male, not impulsive, had no financial stress, and no recent losses or separations. Though we had no awareness of this, she must have had acute suicidal ideation. And we know she had acute overuse of alcohol and severe sense of hopelessness. But three of eleven? That did not seem like enough to end her life.

While she may not have had many factors placing her at a high risk for suicide, I came to see that she had almost none of the protective factors that might have prevented her from following through on a suicide. These factors include: children in the home, deterrent religious beliefs, pregnancy, reality testing ability, life satisfaction, positive coping skills, positive social support, and positive therapeutic relationship. She was under severe psychic anxiety and she had little ability to tolerate psychological pain.

* * *

A GREATER PERSPECTIVE

There reaches a point in the middle of grief that is extremely isolating. The immediacy of our loss is gone, but we still feel a great sense of separation from the rest of the world. People begin to get tired of hearing us talk about things and yet the loss is still so forefront in our minds. This preoccupation is a natural part of grieving. I know that for a period I was totally consumed by the event that had precipitated my grief.

For mourners, tremendous amounts of energy are spent on grief. As a normal and natural reaction to loss, we travel the entire range of naturally occurring human emotions in a short time, which can be an exhausting business. As a result, we feel both more vulnerable and more tired than we did before, and than those around us.

During this time, I know I could talk and think of almost nothing but my loss. I was a new person in a foreign world, and I was still trying to get used to it. My old life was completely over. I was still here in the same surroundings and the same body, but with a completely different perspective, and I was still not entirely sure what that perspective was yet. Everything old had fallen away. What was left?

I could not connect to the world through my story, but I could connect to life. Just a sense that I was alive, that I had not expired from this great loss felt like something miraculous. That I was surviving was important me, given that my mother had not survived her mental anguish.

And while it seemed so antithetical to the order of nature (it is debatable whether animals commit suicide, and they certainly don't use firearms to do it), her death did not upset the workings of nature. There was something so comforting in that. The world did not stop. It just absorbed it. Life went on. If the universe could absorb it, then maybe somehow so could I. Maybe it meant that the world was not turned upside down, only my perspective was.

The eleventh gift of grief is a sense of connection to and comfort in being alive, and human. We appreciate life more for our having experienced another's loss of it. We can find comfort and safety in ourselves. This heartbeat contemplation helped me to surrender to a greater sense of life in the universe, the one that can absorb everything, even our worst nightmares.

* * *

ANTIDOTE TO GRIEF
11. Heartbeat contemplation:
An antidote to desolation

HEARTBEAT CONTEMPLATION

The goal of life is to make your heartbeat match the beat of the universe, your nature with nature. ~ Joseph Campbell

Find your own pulse on your neck. Or notice the heartbeat in your chest. Can you feel the pulse running through your hands? Become aware of your heartbeat. The rhythm of it- the speed. Does it change? Place your full attention on it, on the life moving through you. Now bring your attention to the breath, and the cycle of the breath. Notice the combination of the two life rhythms moving through you. Watch the two rhythms interact- a symphony of aliveness in your body, happening in each moment. Now bring your awareness again to the beating of your heart. Notice the heartbeat itself, and the space between beats. Notice the larger space in which the heartbeat happens, the larger space through which life moves.

12

GRATITUDE

When you change the way you look at things, the things you look at change.
~Wayne Dyer

THE STORY

When someone we love dies, we want to know that his or her life had meaning. We want to feel that they were good; that they somehow made a difference; that they left the world a better place. I found this difficult because of the moral implications of my mother's suicide. I wasn't sure how or if to judge her for what she had done, and at times I could not help myself from falling into the unconscious trap of feeling some kind of absurd vengefulness toward her for all of the pain she had left behind.

For a time, I could not see the difference she made on the world because of the stain she had left as she departed. Should a person's life be judged on the manner of their death? Should a person's life be judged at all? What kind of mark is it on your character when you murder yourself?

The choice to take one's life is indicative of free will; one thing that most people agree is a right of man. However, taking a human life is seen by many as the ultimate sin, making suicide a topic that has been debated throughout the ages. It has been characterized as cowardly, weak, sinful, shameful, demonstrating a frailty of character, and, conversely, under certain conditions, greatly courageous. We unconsciously carry with us these opinions about self-slaughter. In his book, Suicide and the Soul, James Hillman writes, *"the tension of body and soul is crystallised most clearly in the problem of suicide. Here, the body can be destroyed by a 'mere fantasy'. No other question forces us so acutely into facing the reality of the psyche as a reality equal to the body"*. [7]

Moral philosophers approach the questions of right and wrong from the perspective of consequences. The degree of negative consequences for other people determines the moral question of an act. Do the negative consequences of the action more than outweigh the positive effect? If suicide could be morally judged by the consequences it has for others, then it felt to me among the worst things one could do.

In addition to wondering whether and how to judge my mother for what she had done, for me, the moral aspects of suicide and its accompanying stigma contributed to a feeling of deep isolation from the rest of the world as I mourned. This was augmented by the fact that when others approached me to offer condolences, they came with their own confusion. People felt they needed to have something to say to ease the general moral uncertainty, and their approach ranged from avoiding the topic entirely to intense curiosity; from referring to my mother as an athlete going out on top of her game to comparing her to a wise monk who had the foresight to know that her time on earth was over. People told me she was classy, courageous, advised me to ignore it, and, most troubling, expressed congratulations on her bravery and a wish that they had the strength to do such a thing themselves.

Though I do not take it personally, it still touches a vulnerable spot whenever anyone makes a casual suicide reference- some examples being the childhood game of wall ball, also called 'suicide'; the gunshot to the head gesture; gun pop in the mouth; the expressions, *Just shoot me now, if I have to do that again I am going to shoot myself in the head, kill myself, take a gun to my head, stick a gun in my mouth.* I hadn't realized what a basic part of our lexicon suicide is and how much we unconsciously take for granted our right to kill ourselves when the going gets tough.

When I thought about this, I also felt that the fact that people refer to suicide as a choice was misleading. Choice implies that a suicidal person can reasonably look at alternatives and select among them. If they could rationally choose, it would not be suicide. Suicide happens when no other choices are seen. Still, I was aware that for my own part, I had been introduced in a very direct way to this as a new "*choice*" in my life, because as a professional I knew that at some point, most survivors contemplate thoughts of suicide themselves. Despite how I felt about my own mother's suicide, I still wanted to reserve this "*right*" for myself.

* * *

A GREATER PERSPECTIVE

Moral confusion is present with all loss, though it manifests in different ways, and it accounts for the isolation that we feel from other people, and to a general feeling that they don't understand what we are going through. We approach mourners in different ways, depending upon whether they have lost a child or a parent; on whether the one who died had cancer or was murdered; whether the death was untimely; a sudden accident; or by design. Still, part and parcel with mourning comes the sense that because each individual and relationship is so unique, there is a part of this journey we must walk alone.

There are certain aspects of our grief that no one may ever understand. No matter how much support we receive, it is us alone that must make room for the agony of the loss. When we give ourselves space to experience this loneliness we might be prevented from becoming overwhelmed by it by recognizing that it is only one aspect of our mourning. Just behind our sense of isolation is the universal human understanding that loss is an intimate part of every living thing.

The twelfth gift of grief is a reconnection to the gift of life, its preciousness and precariousness. This sense of aliveness is all the richer for our having temporarily lost our connection to it, and for someone else's loss of life. When can feel and honor this sense of life's fragility and preciousness, we are left with a sense of connection to all life. Gratitude of Life contemplation, connecting us with all life, can help us stay joined with our gratitude for this life and all that it offers us.

* * *

ANTIDOTE TO GRIEF
12. Gratitude of life meditation:
An antidote to isolation

GRATITUDE OF LIFE CONTEMPLATION

Begin by focusing on the breath. Access a sense of gratefulness for this greater intelligence behind the breath, which continues to tie us to life with each inhale and exhale. Become aware of this greater intelligence at work in the body. Be aware of your eyes. Give thanks for eyes that can see all of the wonders of the universe, and your ears, which can hear the most exquisite sound. Notice your lungs. The lungs breathe even as we sleep. It is wonderful to have health in our lungs and our inner organs. Continue to bring your grateful awareness to all of the wonderful working parts of your body. Find the places that gently rest on one another in whatever position you are in. Let the touch of your limbs to one another be like an embrace to your inner being. Feel gratitude for your hands and feet.

Now connect with the aliveness in every living thing, even the smallest insect. Feel the fragility, and preciousness, the value of every life, no matter how short or small. Give thanks for your favorite people, animals, and plants. Thank the earth for holding you up; for sustaining and supporting all living things in a perfect design. With open arms toward the sky, finish your meditation saying to the universe: Thank you for this life.

13

COMPASSION

*What lies behind us and what lies before us are but
tiny matters compared to what lies within us.*
~Ralph Waldo Emerson

THE STORY

To survive a loved one's suicide without being decimated by it, we eventually need to become very comfortable with uncertainty and the unanswerable. People spend a great deal of time trying to track down causes, precipitating factors, character vulnerabilities, and the exact epidemiology of this plague upon our house. We may fool ourselves into thinking that we have it all sewn up, that we know the reasons why this occurred. Much of this is false bravado, an attempt to convince ourselves that we won't catch the same affliction that took our loved one away.

The deep desire to fend off this ending for ourselves takes different forms for different people. Some people turn away from the mystery completely, denying the suicide at all. They are too uncomfortable with what they associate with a frailty of character to allow themselves to think about it at all. One acquaintance, whose sister had committed suicide, summed it all up in one answer, *That's what happens when you don't take your meds!* I could hear the pain and anger in her voice. We all may be speaking a part of the truth, but the greater whole is that making peace with suicide is a lot like dying itself: without having experienced it directly we will never know for sure. The more comfortable we are with this unexplainable mystery, the more peace we will find about the reality of it.

Regarding our own family journey, we were ending the phase of trying to figure out and understand the circumstances leading directly up to my mother's death, but our family therapy led us further back into our family's past. In looking through old photos and emails, I came across two things. The first was an email written by my mother from India nine months before her suicide. The fall before her death, just one year ago, she was writing cheerful letters about her amazing experiences and adventures (see Appendix VII for letter). Still traveling, still connected and curious about the world and the people in it, a year later she was so distraught that she could not keep herself alive. How quickly things could change, an insight I found both terrifying and uplifting.

The second thing was the last picture taken of her, at a party she attended just weeks before she died, only nine months after she had written that email, wearing the brightest fuschia, standing close to my father with a graceful look on her face. In the photo, I compared her public face to what she had told me about that party (that she had stayed too long and had a very bad day the next day). I recalled what medication she was on- just switched, by phone, to Lexiprau off of Prozac and was about 5 days on. It was not working and she had a strong feeling that the Prozac had "poisoned" her system because it had made her so sick and felt it was in some way responsible for her worsening depression as well. She was desperate for a new medication to work *immediately*. She had not started seeing Dr. F yet. She had not yet bought the gun; there was still hope.

At that party she was really at the end of her rope. The hot pink shirt seems like her last bold effort to fly in the face of the blackness she felt inside, like waving a red flag at a bull. And yet there she is in the photo, acting the part that everyone down there had come to expect of her and loved her so much for- the consummately bred woman- taste, manners, charity, humor.

I was overcome by the juxtaposition of someone's public face and their private torment. I sat in the airport on the way home, struck fully in the chest, my heart raw and aching, with the deep realization that everyone, each person I passed, carried around a secret pain all of their own. I felt connected to it all, and experienced a oneness simultaneously painful and comforting.

Somehow that last photo I found of her makes it clear to me just how desperate she was to escape, as William Styron describes it in his account of depression, this *howling tempest in the brain*. She was exhausted, tired of the self raging, self destructive monster that she had been trying to hide all of these years, but by trying to hide it it grew in her mind, grew to unmanageable proportions, and this became too much for her. So she decided to kill it. She planned a murder; the murder of her mind. She committed suicide, literally murdering the *"self"*. Unfortunately in doing so she also took her life. My mother had missed the point. She had wanted to kill her psyche, not herself.

* * *

A GREATER PERSPECTIVE

In the process of complex grief, the noise of emotions and the constant motion of thoughts can be completely overwhelming. This can be exacerbated by the extreme state of sensitivity that often accompanies grief. At times, it can actually feel like we may not survive it. In my own process, as I withstood what felt like the unbearable, it was unbelievably helpful to have something to focus on, some larger connection to life besides the process going on in my head.

However, staying with that discomfort without becoming lost in it is the key to mining one of the greatest gifts of grief. Each time we are genuine with ourselves and what we actually experience in a moment and not what we wish were happening, each time we recognize the humanness of our situation, it accumulates to the kind of inner strength that we need to live in this challenging world. It also leads us to compassion, or a feeling of deep empathy for anyone who is stricken by misfortune, and a wish to alleviate their suffering.

A heightened sense of compassion for all life, and for the universal anguish of grief that is experienced by every living thing, is something that most grievers experience. It allows us to expand as human beings, by bringing us beyond our own story to connect with something greater than ourselves. The story of our pain may feel unique, but it is matched by millions of other stories of pain and suffering on the planet. Only when we are in the midst of this deep pain can we truly appreciate, empathize with, and have a strong desire to assuage another's distress.

The thirteenth gift of grief is true compassion, a sense of deep connection and empathy with all living, suffering beings. Out of our own deep misery, we recognize both how human and how universal our suffering is. The breath of life contemplation, in addition to helping us to connect to something larger than our own suffering, keeps us connected to our humanness. With each breath, it literally allows us to choose life. The thin thread that separates us from life and death and connects us to all living, breathing beings can always be found in the breath.

* * *

ANTIDOTE TO GRIEF
13. Breath of Life Contemplation:

An antidote to oversensitivity

BREATH OF LIFE CONTEMPLATION

The mind can go in many different directions in a split second. The breath has only one path- inhalation & exhalation.
~ Iyengar

Tune into the larger intelligence at work in the breath. Breath happens all day long, all of our lives, without our being aware of it. Without it we would not have life. It is one of the very first things we do as we enter the world, and it is one of the last things we will do as we exit. Become aware of the breath. Tune into the feeling of it entering your body at each different point- your nose, your throat, your lungs. Stay with one inbreath and one outbreath- keep all of your awareness on it. Now try it again. Use the breath as your focal point, or mantra. Constantly bring yourself back to your inbreath, then your outbreath. Notice the space between your inbreath & outbreath. Notice the space in which your breath happens.

Allow the breath of life to flow through you, so it is not so much about you breathing as it is about life breathing through you. Feel life breathing through you and all around you like a warm breeze enveloping you in its aliveness. Allow yourself to follow the flow of life's breath as it moves across and within your body- within your heart center and lungs as they expand. You may notice an increased feeling of aliveness in your body as the breath of life flows through you. Allow the breath of consciousness to move across your pain, softening it the way a warm summer breeze tempers everything in its path. As you go through your day, keep some of your attention on the breath moving through you.

14

STEPPING OUTSIDE OF TIME

If you can be absolutely comfortable with not knowing who you are, then what's left is who you are - the Being behind the human, a field of pure potentiality rather than something that is already defined. Give up defining yourself - to yourself and others. You won't die. You will come to life.
~ Eckhart Tolle

THE STORY

When she was alive, my mother had become a fixed impression for me, perpetually present. Especially toward the end of her life, she seemed often to be holding or acting out a tension that was either subtle or overt- through dry wit, irritation, or outright anger. My conditioned image of her was never as a sympathetic character. In fact the last time I saw her I felt the opposite of sympathy toward her. As I pulled out of the driveway, I could see her through my rearview mirror standing solidly at the end in a goodbye gesture, and all I could feel was relief at getting away from her and the tension I felt toward her. I saw that she was falling apart and I was angry with her for it.

But this suicide was off the charts- way out of the realm of any image I had of mother. My mother was gone- not just literally but figuratively as well. I had to let go of my old imprint of her- so solid in my mind. In a new way, I became acutely aware that she had an inner life, one much more complex than I had ever thought.

I try to make my more recent perceptions of her less flat. Looking back more carefully, when was the last time I saw her happy? Had I ever even asked myself that question? I never thought about her as happy or unhappy. Just when had she gone from my silent, strong, sometimes scary mother to my silent suffering mother? Had she always been that way?

In psychological training, we learn that our most formative impressions, and therefore our deepest wounds, are felt in the first seven years of our lives. Most of the pain that we feel after this is just an unconscious repetition, in some form, of these first primitive responses. Seen from this perspective, then, my mother must have learned self-hatred and repression in her first seven years. The seeds of her suicide were sewn then.

I can only speculate about specifics. With regard to her parents, she was not fighting the demons of physical abuse but the lack of love she felt and her resultant sense of unworthiness. No amount of exterior abundance could compensate for her inner perception of unworthiness. In her depressive breakdown, I remember her saying to me; *I have no reason to feel so awful. I have a wonderful life! A beautiful house, wonderful children, grandchildren. I shouldn't feel so horrible.* On the outside, she was a woman that most people envied- a woman who had it all.

Much of what I know about my mother's early life was interpreted through her. About her own mother she expressed intimidation, fear of her anger, and a derision of her constant anxiety. Of her father, I think she held a quiet love coupled with disappointment in his constant drunkenness.

On the outside, it was a world of polished beauty: crisp lawned country clubs and duplex apartments in the city; family trips to exclusive ranches in the west; private schools and summers in Maine. Outwardly pristine, under the surface there was an unconscious dysfunction. Alcohol played a major role in this. My mother's was a good-natured WASP family filled with amazing intelligence, humor, and self-deprecation, and unfortunately laden with a heavy propensity for alcoholism.

When I was a child, going to visit my grandparents brought about an atmosphere in our house of tightly held to-gether unexpressed emotions, the long lunches at country clubs to be endured politely and quietly, strong emotions and words associated with them to be always repressed, a process described by my mother as white knuckling it. Her tension leading up to these events was overt and filled the house. I re-member feeling that we were expected to be dressed in beauti-ful preppy clothes, be cheerful but not loud, and to generally stay out of the way.

When my mother was around the age of three, she was separated from her parents for two years after an accident in which my grandfather was hit by a horse and carriage, leaving him without the ability to walk or talk. During the long process of rehabilitation, my mother was sent to live with her grand-mother. Certainly a separation from one's parents at that age of development would be traumatizing, and it could doubtless leave a young child with a sense of deep abandonment.

When she was sixteen, my mother was raped by an em-ployee while on vacation at a ranch in Montana. She told this to my sister Miranda late one drunken night, and she reported that it was the only time her parents ever hugged her or told her they loved her. Then they told her never to speak of it again. My father reports that when she was twenty, just before they met, she was date raped by a local peer, who apparently had a reputation for it. My grandfather went to his house wav-ing a shotgun, but charges were never pressed against the man. Soon after, she and my father were married.

Both of my parents' families are a long line of White An-glo-Saxon Protestants. Within this culture is a list of unspoken rules and unconscious assumptions. When I was very young, I remember my mother commenting, always with sarcasm, that, *in my family, the men go to Harvard, and the women get married.* There were certain tacit rules in our family. First, never show your true feelings. Keep things hidden. And always look and act like everything was just fine.

As such, my mother's alcoholism was not the loud bois-terous embarrassing type. She didn't spill into people's laps or put a lampshade on her head at parties. Hers was the secret kind, which she worked hard to hide from everyone. She had numerous occasions throughout her life when she tried to quit drinking on her own and succeeded for periods of time. After she spent a month in rehab in 1988, which was a more public effort, she never drank in front of others, and there was a part of herself that she increasingly hid from the world. It came out late at night, when she thought everyone was asleep and she might spare them the true measure of her pain. She held her-self in all day and only released her demons to herself when alone and in the dark.

As a child, she appeared to me to be both enchanting and rather frightening: a larger than life figure who could act men-acingly in some moments and magically in others. She was a hard to fathom, impossible to touch person, whom I was al-ways either pushing against or trying to commune with. In the best moments, being with my mother was like being immersed in a captivating fairytale. She bestowed her sense of life's won-der in creative and irresistable ways.

To love an alcoholic is like an addiction itself. At times, life with my mother was like being blanketed in a world of magical surprises, wonder, and a feeling of love beyond meas-ure. It was a cool drink, a day in the shade looking up at the trees against the sky. It was feast or famine. Soaked or scorched. When the enchanted quilt came down upon you, it was worth any amount of days or years spent searching and lost in the parched desert trying to find it. I can see that on an unconscious level my whole adulthood has been about trying to recreate these moments.

I recognize that the fragility that initially made her turn toward alcohol for relief was also what made my mother so extraordinary. The attempt to cover up that vulnerability is what made her so funny. Her deep desire to fend off her suffering was what made her grab the celebration in life with such captivating force. Without these elements she would have been a completely different person.

* * *

A GREATER PERSPECTIVE

The thing that can be so difficult about grief is that for every mourner, the trajectory of their story is changed irrevocably, and not in a longed for direction. Our stories are our identities and when we lose them, we can feel a literal cavity. This causes the sense of depression that is a part of grief.

In grief, the depression we feel is less clinical and more like a despondency, or a feeling of dispiritedness. This can occur when we finally realize the true magnitude of our loss. In the emptiness, at first we may only feel despair, or a sense of panic at not knowing how to define ourselves anymore. If we are not our history, who are we?

In my own case, I liken this confused period, when I was coming to terms with a new reality, to the disjointedness that often occurs just before the jumping forward to a new phase of development. In developmental psychology, experts (Erikson, Ames & Ames) notice a period of organization and disorganization in each developmental phase. In spiritual terms, this period of confusion follows an experience of enlightenment. I had experienced both a decimation of my life as I understood it and also some moments of the deepest beauty and connection I had ever known. For me, there was no past story to cling to. All I had was the present moment. But instead of experiencing this as liberating, at first I felt a kind of disorientation, as if I were stuck between the past and the future. Buddhists refer to this as getting stuck in emptiness- detached from the drama but no connection to the here and now. It is not necessarily negative but more initially disconcerting.

At the same time that it is unsettling, the place it brings us to is a sense of timelessness that can only be found in the present. **The fourteenth gift of grief is that it connects us directly to the present moment, where all life is happening.** Present moment contemplation helped me to access a part of myself and of life that was deeper than my story, my history, or my pain. From a different perspective, this sense of disorientation could also be felt as a full sense of timelessness. In the end, getting stuck between the past and the future is actually very liberating, because it places us squarely in the present moment, and when we connect with it, we realize that all life is truly happening in the now.

* * *

ANTIDOTE TO GRIEF
14. Present Moment Contemplation:
An antidote to disorientation

PRESENT MOMENT CONTEMPLATION: WHO ARE YOU REALLY?

No matter who you are, no matter how old you are,
in the present all things are possible.~ Marianne Williamson

Find a quiet place to sit in stillness. Imagine for a moment that you have no name. Imagine that you have no history, no life story. What is left of you? Awareness. Feel your breath as it enters and exits. Feel the sensations in the inner body. Feel the greater life flowing through you. Get in touch with a part of you that is beyond your thoughts, beyond the personal. This is who you really are. Spend some time in this greater awareness. Focus a soft attitude on the unnameable part of yourself. As you watch your breath, ask yourself who is doing the breathing? Find the source of your awareness. From where does your awareness originate? To what is it connected outside of your body?

Concentrate on this very moment and the world that lies within it- the sounds, sensed movement, sensations. Don't name them, just sense them. Pretend for a moment that there is no past or future. Imagine this moment is all you have. There is no past, no future, just this moment. Become absolutely awake, absolutely still, so you don't miss any part of it. If thoughts occur, notice them and then bring your attention back to now. Something could happen at any moment and if you are not absolutely aware, you will miss it, and it will be gone forever. Enter a new state of waiting, becoming intensely conscious of this moment to see all that it holds. This moment *is* all that you have.

Practice experiencing this moment with your entire awareness. Listen with your whole being, as if your toes and feet could hear what is being said. Experience now with your open heart. Allow every nerve ending to practice being receptive to the now. Hold your attention on the moment as it happens, not jumping forward to a response, not guessing ahead at what might happen, but staying with the moment itself, journeying with each moment as it comes into being, and letting each one fall away as it passes. Be the container for the moment. Take the moment in with your whole being. Allow space for life to unfold. Let there be space for all of it in this greater awareness that is you.

15

FLEXIBILITY

*We shall not cease from exploration, and the end of all our exploring will be to arrive
where we started and know the place for the first time. ~ T.S. Eliot*

*Dear Mom, How did we get so far away from each other?
I was always pushing against you, trying to find me.*

THE STORY

When we lose someone, we are oftentimes grieving as
much for what we didn't have as for what we did. We mourn
the loss of possibility for this person to be all that they could,
to achieve peace. We regret the end of the potential for our
relationship.

Grieving my mother involved mourning the loss of a relationship that I had always wished for with her. Taking a
more conscious look at what our relationship had been and
not just what I hoped it would be was a challenging process. It
required me to look more deeply into my own early life and
formative years, which began with a cultural myth in which I
had come to believe as well.

On the outside, we were the family that everyone wanted
to be like. We were the four Hunt girls with our pretty names
and blonde hair, our summers in Maine and our weekends in
the big old family house in Wisconsin. We would bring our
friends up there to parade around in my grandmother's fancy
evening dresses and tiny shoes and then dance around the living room to "The Flight of the Bumblebee" on the old Victro-
la.

The myth that surrounded families like this produced a
golden halo that many could not see beyond. In the sunset of
WASP dominance, people still idealized this lifestyle, which

they imagined consisted of endless prosperity, privilege, and satisfaction, and delight. We all want to believe in such images because they give us a sense of hope and something to live up to. However, underneath I think there is a recognition that this can't really be the whole truth. No one is happy all the time. The other part of the story contains the truth of what we have suspected all along; that beneath the sheen and perfection of the surface of all lives are shadowy secrets and more complicated realities. In other words, each one of us is all too human, no matter how it may appear.

My mother's demons became more prominent by the time I was around 12, and I can mark my summers of childhood from that time by whether she was having a good summer or a bad one, meaning had alcohol gotten the better of her or not. I remember a renaissance the summer of my wedding, when she turned 50 and displayed an inner resolve and sense of potential that was contagious. I always felt so lucky for this. In pictures of that time, you can see the pure joy of life and new possibilities alight on her face, and my father always staring at her with something like adoration.

The second child of four, I came during the time in between when it was all still lovely and when the dark secrets of my mother's pain and the resulting dance with alcohol began to slip out into foggy afternoons closeted with books and cigarettes with us to fend for ourselves, uncontrollable rages, and all of the pain that someone's unexpressed inner suffering can wreak on a family. I lived in a world that alternated from being comfortable, happy, and exciting to one that was scary and uncertain, and I was not always sure which one I would encounter as I walked in the door from school. Like many middle children, I learned early to walk on the razor's edge, living between these two extremes.

By the time my older sister Julia and I left home for boarding school, things were deteriorating at home. To my sister Miranda, the third, (who, because she so reminded my mother of herself, bore the biggest emotional brunt of my mother's disease), and my youngest sister, life must at times have felt like something of a war zone. From her infancy my youngest sister was mostly raised by our live-in maid, Anna, who took care of us increasingly often, because both my mother and father realized that during certain periods my mother should not be left alone with her children.

As a young child, I remember my mother as an elusive figure, often just out of reach. This may be best illustrated by a recurring dream I had throughout my childhood: I am at the school fair and a fire breaks out. The ground of the gym begins to give way and sway beneath my feet. I know I need to run fast to escape this disaster, but my feet will not move-suddenly they have become impossibly heavy and slow. It is like trying to run with giant blocks of heavy cement for shoes. Fire is chasing me, almost enveloping me completely. I finally make it out of the school to find my mother, sitting on the brick loggia just outside. *Mom!* I scream. *Help me! There's a fire in there! I was so scared! I couldn't get out! I tried to run but my legs wouldn't move! We need to get away now! Hurry!!* My mother is looking at me but doesn't see me. She isn't hearing what I am saying either. She regards me with a dreamy expression, in her own world. She does not recognize the urgency, and no matter how hard I try, I cannot get her to move from her position.

Growing up, the predominant negative feeling of my early childhood was a fear and concern about not fitting in, a reluctance to explore or express myself, and a desire to see and bring about the reappearance of my happy mother no matter what the cost. I in turn learned to hide my emotions from myself so well that as an adult it took me many years to figure out how I was feeling in a moment, or to allow myself to authentically experience the moment without trying to force what I should be feeling or how I should be acting onto it. One message I took from my particular upbringing, from my extended family of origin, was that life was about sacrificing yourself to accommodate someone else. It was about molding yourself to fit in, even if you knew all the while that you didn't.

These more painful family aspects coexisted with an amazing amount of conviviality. A family working so hard to push away the negative experiences no shortage of fun and enjoyment. The closest memories I have of intimacy with my mother are in the things she gave me. While direct words of affection were not common to her, her loving gestures came in the form of gifts, and these were numerous. Her generosity provided abundant opportunities for togetherness through family trips, travel, and shared meals. Laughter was a way of diffusing strong emotions, so there was a lot of joking and banter in our family, in good times and bad. As a family friend once observed, we did fun well.

I took myself to boarding school at age fifteen. I talked to my parents once a week and didn't see them until Thanksgiving. I think my parents thought this was normal. Though she did not say it often, I feel certain that my mother missed me deeply, though it makes me sad to think of whether or how much she allowed herself to admit to or process these feelings.

For me high school was spent trying to figure out a way to fit in and testing out all kinds of identities, looking for love and attention and success anywhere I could find it. The best thing about that time is that I met my husband during that time, and learned about love and kindness on a deeper level. Living on my own, I only just got myself through college, and when I had no idea what to do afterward, I fell into therapy, which helped lead me to graduate school, finding a profession, and having a family.

Despite the complications of our relationship, I adored my mother, and with time, I came to appreciate her for what she could offer when she could offer it. She was generous, charming, and bitingly funny. She didn't meddle in my life or try to control me in any way. She was fun to travel with and taught us and made us feel like life was a big adventure to be enjoyed. She was a fantastic grandmother, and underneath it all, I knew she had deep love for me and that any faults I saw in her were just the things that made her, like the rest of us, all too human.

* * *

A GREATER PERSPECTIVE

In The Little Prince, St. Exupery writes, *"It is the time you have devoted to your rose that makes your rose so important."* This is true of our story. Grief requires flexibility, an ability to adapt to new surroundings. In order for us to move beyond our history, or our background, it is often necessary for us to revisit it. We revisit the story to get a greater perspective- to recognize who we are beyond that. I know that for me, because of the new and sudden ending to this first half of my life, this took a long time to integrate.

While this process feels forced upon us, bringing with it a sense of anger and resistance, it is actually life requiring us to expand. The change in life is what moves us. How we adapt to it is what forms our character. Or as my father said, *I didn't expect to be dealt this hand, but there are some things I can make of it that I might not have before.*

Though we certainly would not have chosen the means by which it comes about, there is a kind of liberation that comes with having everything fall apart. It is a fresh start. We lose some things which we would never have wished to be parted from, but we also leave behind some things that we will never miss because they were never authentically us.

The fifteenth gift of grief is that it broadens our frame of reference on life, teaching us flexibility. We watch ourselves adapt. We expand, and in doing so, we are greatly strengthened.

* * *

ANTIDOTE TO GRIEF
15. Flexibility: An antidote to resistance

<u>TREE CONTEMPLATION: FLEXIBILITY</u>

If we surrendered to earth's intelligence we could rise up rooted, like trees.
~ *Rainer Maria Rilke*

Begin by feeling the sensations in the inner energy field of the body. Just notice what is present in the body. Turn your attention from your thoughts the experience of your aliveness in the body. Now imagine a tree. You are the tree, rooted in the ground, with branches reaching out until they merge with the space around them. Feel your own energy like that of a tree, flexible but solid, rooted in being. Life is drawn up from the ground through the center of your being and spread it to the tips of your fingers. There is no effort in the tree. There is so resistance. The branches are not fighting with one another. Notice the complete lack of resistance, and the overall energy, solid and malleable at the same time. Even in a huge wind, while the branches may swing about wildly, the root of the tree remains solid in the ground, connected to something greater than itself. As the seasons of the tree's life progress, notice the continual cycles of death and rebirth. The environment is in constant change and motion, but the essence of the tree remains the same.

PART THREE:

EMBODIMENT

16

PERSPECTIVE

Attempting to decipher precisely the thoughts of the suicide victim is much like trying to understand a foreign language by eavesdropping on a conversation. You can analyze the sounds and syllables all day long, but it's not likely you're going to understand much of what was said. Based on the accounts of those who have attempted suicide and lived to tell about it, we know that the primary goal of a suicide is not to end life, but to end pain. People in the grips of a suicidal depression are battling an emotional agony that, to them, is so severe as to make dying a less objectionable alternative than living.

One of the more painful emotions felt by survivors comes when we try to empathize with the severity of this pain. We try to envision what we would have to feel to make the same choice, and when we imagine our loved one in that kind of pain it's almost too much to even consider."~ Jeffrey Jackson, Suicide Survivor's Handbook, American Association of Suicidology

THE STORY

When someone commits suicide, it opens a door for everyone in the family. For my family, what might have seemed unfathomable was now a roadmap that had been left to us by the most important figure in our lives. Our mother was the centrifugal force around which we all spun. That she had murdered herself left us vulnerable to a new kind of dying. In fact, they say that in families who have experienced suicide, the suicide rate goes up by 50%. Like an unwanted disease, suicide had entered our lives without permission and would stay with us forever as a reality. The ultimate challenging question for all of us became, will we exit the world the way our mother did?

I answered this question for myself in the spring after my mother died. I knew there was a part of me that was floundering in grief- not just letting it pass but making it stronger with thoughts and feelings. I spent a lot of time in bed. Days and weeks passed without me leaving the comfort of my room during the hours when my son was at school. This wallowing had a different characteristic from raw pain, in that there was a part of my mind that was almost gratified by it, and would seek to make it stronger with aggravating thinking patterns.

I recognized an unconscious desire to put myself in my mother's shoes by trying to experience as much pain as I imagined she was in when she killed herself. I was trying to commune with her somehow by identifying with her. I wondered how much suffering could a person endure. At what point would suicidality kick in? I had felt the danger of walking on this ground, but there was also a part of me that needed to know.

The lowest point came in the shower around the time of my birthday, so inexorably tied to motherhood. I felt such a huge rejection on that front. My mother gave birth to me, and yet she also chose to leave me. This felt like such an enormous weight. Would it ever not feel this way? I just could not get beyond the reality of my own mother losing her will to live, not to stay for me. Her love for me should have been enough to make her want to live.

All children have this innate need to feel that they are the causal factor of their parent's love for them. All parents have this amazing love for their children over themselves. I would gladly die to save my son. What happened to my mother's instincts?

She had exited this life, left her children and family, by choice. I felt broken and completely without the strength to go on in reaction to these painful thoughts. When absorbed like this, I could relate with a part of her that might have just become too tired to go on in the face of so much pain. And then anger flooded into me. The lives our parents live are the closest thing we have to a blueprint for getting through life. I was so angry at being left behind with such a horrible map to follow.

The rage and agitation I felt led me to a stream of thinking that went something like this. *How could she do this to us? She chose this. I don't care what state she was in. She left Dad. She abandoned him and all of us- just cut out. Then committed violent murder. On herself. This is literally the worst thing anyone could do to anyone else. The worst burden to leave someone with. It's worse than being murdered- at least when you are murdered you didn't consciously choose it. But we are left here to suffer her act. These repercussions should be hers, they came from her, and yet we suffer them. Over and over during her life ran from her pain. And I could forgive her all of that. But not this. This is the worst of all. Suicide: the ultimate insult. And a gun, the most violent form of offense: to run away not just from your pain, but from your consequences, too. That's sick. I would never ever do that to my child. But here's my mother, saying, Hey, I took the low road- and in the end, the very lowest road of all- but now you stay here, with no healthy blueprint, no good example, and do it right- figure it out, take the high road. I don't care about her pain. I don't care who she was in the end- fallen and alone. I just want to hate her.*

I remember standing in the shower and allowing myself to fall into this thinking, wondering where it would take me. There was a logic to my thoughts and yet clearly they were amping up my agitation. Somehow this felt animating, like I was finally fully connected to life again, even if it was an angry contact. Part of me surrendered to the feelings and part of me was cogitating in response to them and part of me was observing all of it with a sense of detachment, wondering where this intense suffering would take me.

In response to this passion I wanted to hurt someone, something. The idea of cutting my wrists, watching the blood slide down my arms, mixing with the water, feeling the relief, the revenge- what vindication it would be. This is what she felt- the rage, and the sense that this would somehow show everyone, even though it would decimate her.

And then my next thought came. Could I sustain this impulse? Could I wait nine days and still do this? Impossible. I could see the frenzy of the moment, and being overcome. I could not see the foresight or planning.

At this realization a sudden great calm came over me. The thoughts stopped and I let the shower water wash over me with a sense of relief deep in my being. I was immersed in suffering, but this was where our paths diverged. I would never end my life in the way my mother did. I felt the difference between us now thoroughly. And I could still feel great tenderness and compassion for this woman. In order to love her, I did not need to identify with her in this way. I experienced a sense of security like a warm covering.

Connected with this tranquility was a deep enchantment I had not felt for a long time. It was like I had been plugged back in to life. I could feel a way to be with this pain without it destroying me. Sometimes, like today, it might feel like it would engulf me. Other days, it would be way below the surface; so far that I could feel light again, enough to even forget about it. Everything passes. I could look ahead and see things changing.

I had reached my lowest point and not expired. Once again the image of breaking through the sky into a new place came to me. I was elated while at the same time peaceful, and also still with this great pain about my mother. There was room for all of it. It felt like the description from the Tibetan Book of Living and Dying, *"as though pain and pleasure are occurring at the same time, or a powerful shower of icy cold water and boiling hot water is pouring simultaneously over your body."* [8].

* * *

A GREATER PERSPECTIVE

When I was in the shower, I recognized three different parts of myself: a sense of extreme pain; the thoughts and emotions occurring in reaction to the pain; and a witness that seemed to have some overall perspective on things and could see how the thoughts I was indulging myself in were exacerbating the pain until it became unbearable. A grieving part of me needed to take myself as far down the suffering road as I could to try and relate with my mother until I reached the point where our paths diverged. I now knew for certain I would never end things in the manner she did, for I had something she had lost: perspective.

Anger is a very big part of the grieving process. At some point, there is universal sense of unfairness about what happened. We ask ourselves why us? What did we do to deserve this? We may look for someone or something to blame. The questions we ask ourselves only exacerbate things. Eventually what will bring clarity is recognizing the difference between our pain and our suffering. If we stay with the pain and diligently look for a different perspective on it, it can become a strengthening and clarifying force in our lives.

One of the traps of grief is that we can fall into the identity of the victim. When this happens, we have mistaken our suffering for who we are. Many spiritual teachings address this. For example, the saying in Buddhism is, *don't identify yourself as a crippled person*. What keeps us from getting stuck in this pitfall are practices that allow us to experience ourselves as much more than our suffering.

Working with emotional pain requires bravery. We are faced with all of the things about life that we thought we could not tolerate. However, in his book The Tibetan Book of Living and Dying, the Dalai Lama states, "*As long as we are not freed from the bonds of the disturbing emotions, it is impossible to obtain real and secure happiness*". [9] In order to do this, he advises, don't bond yourself to the painful emotions you are experiencing. Don't try to attach yourself to them, distance yourself from, or deny them. Just let them pass through.

No matter where we have become trapped in grief, there is always room for change. The teachings of Tibetan Buddhism have at their base a core belief that each one of us is made up of basic goodness which can always be accessed. Renowned Tibetan Buddhist monk and teacher Pema Chodron describes that no matter how far we have fallen in terms of emotions or life circumstances, no matter how much suffering we have experienced, it in no way touches our fundamental goodness. It is another way of saying, never give up on yourself. One thing that makes this process easier for mourners is that there is a kind of inner stubbornness that we access during deep grief. Sometimes referred to as survival mode, it is an instinct that keeps us going and able to walk through things we never thought we could tolerate.

When we access our basic goodness, when we move beyond the place of fear, there is enormous potential. This is how we take pain and turn it into medicine. This is the ultimate antidote to grief. When we stay awake enough to ride the waves of pain to their natural end without being overtaken by them, we can reap the reward of the true recognition that something inside us is stronger than the pain. Each time we do this, we build a foundation of deep inner strength.

The sixteenth gift of grief is perspective. Through anger comes clarity. The realization that the fog of every emotion eventually clears can help strengthen us the next time a storm of suffering overtakes us. Pain contemplation can assist us to reach this kind of clarity. This particular contemplation is one that I find extremely helpful in times when my negative thoughts are running the show. It is the most useful practice I have experienced for processing emotions without leaving an energetic residue of suffering.

* * *

ANTIDOTE TO GRIEF
16. Pain perspective: An antidote to anger

PAIN CONTEMPLATION

Pain is inevitable. Suffering is optional.
~ Dalai Lama

Sit quietly and connect with your inner body. Notice the breath as it occurs naturally in the body, without our will or direction, or even our attention on it. Now become aware of the greater movement of the moment beyond the body. Notice the noises around you, and connect with the energy of the earth in this particular point of its cycle. Watch the interplay of the flow of the energy inside the body and the natural energies of the planet. As you do this exercise, always keep some of your attention on the connection to your body and breath, and on your connection to the greater universal energy to which you are connected through this moment.

Call to your awareness an emotionally painful experience from your past- you may start with something relatively small. Allow yourself to be there, back in the midst of it, long enough to bring to mind the story, to feel the emotions and the charge around the event. Do not give 100% of your thoughts to the experience- don't become lost in it. Keep some of your attention on the refuge of the space in which these thoughts and emotions are occurring- the present moment. Now ring a bell, or clap your hands, and when you do so, immediately drop the story and stay with the feeling in the inner body. Watch it from a place of awareness. Keep your simple attention on the physical sensations in the body. Feel the quality of your bodily impressions. Don't try and name them, just continue to experience the pure perception of your physical body. If the story comes in, continue to look underneath it and feel the vibration in the physical body.

Now ring the bell or clap your hands again. Bring back the story. Keep your attention on it long enough for the physical response in the body to intensify again. Ring or clap and drop the story again, and stay with what is left. Continue to turn your attention away from your thoughts and toward the accompanying sensations that are present in the body.

Do this one more time. You are making your first steps in learning how to experience pain skillfully. Recognizing the larger space in which your pain is occurring helps you to recognize yourself as more than just the pain. When this happens, subconscious resistance begins to break up, and so does the pain. It starts to flow and shift. It is as though your consciousness were dough and the pain wave is kneading that dough, working out the lumps and the kinks, transforming it at a molecular level into something soft, pliant and malleable.

Finish with an offering of love and kindness toward yourself and all that you experienced; a recognition of the basic goodness that is your core. Sit quietly in the safe haven of the present moment, in your comfortable spot, allowing life and breath to move through you and cradle you with lovingkindness. Before you get up, list three things that you are grateful for and allow yourself to feel this gratitude in your inner energy field. As you go through your day, if the painful event/feelings come back into your consciousness, keep separating the story around the pain and the accompanying emotions from the physical sensations in the body. (This focused attention will keep things flowing and allow the pain to pass.) Keep some connection to the larger space in which this experience is happening.

17

FORGIVENESS

Forgiveness is the fragrance the violet sheds on the heel of the boot that crushes it.
~Mark Twain

~

....The scene through the bow window dissolves and a new one appears.
The woman is in her bedroom, sitting by a little telephone table. She is making
phone calls, to each one of her children. She does not look well. You see the
dark circles under her eyes, the vacant expression, as if a part of her were miss-
ing on the inside. She is trying not to cry, and sometimes her words falter...I'm
not sure how much longer I can go on like this, you can hear her say...she asks
about her grandchildren, expresses, to the best of her ability, enfeebled enthusi-
asm about something one of them has just learned to do. She tries to say some-
thing now: I...I...but she cannot get the words out. She is beginning to cry now.
Soon she hangs up the phone, and slumps over in her seat, exhausted. She lies
down curled up in her place and stops moving....

THE STORY

After my experience in the shower, a certain momentum had returned to my life. I had felt the ultimate juxtaposition- the constantly changing nature of life. One moment, I could experience extreme doubt. In the next, I could be deeply root- ed in a faith in something larger. Things could change in a moment. As Pema Chodron puts it, *things come together and they fall apart- they come together and they fall apart- that is the nature of things. Our job is to let there be room for all of it.*[10]

I knew that I had been absorbed in my misery. The re- cent suffering was my immediate reaction to this painful event. The old suffering had been in storage for years. My intention was to clean out my closet so that I no longer had to step over and around things in order to access the joy in life.

I had been grounded about my mother, without any drive to move forward. A part of what I was looking for some consolation for what I had lost. If I was honest, what I truly wanted was an abject apology and contrition for the pain and mess my mother left behind; some wisdom about the poor choices she made in her life and where they got her; some understanding that her choice of death made it difficult not to see her life as a failure; an understanding that her suicide was not a conscious falling toward the light but rather a running from her own pain, and that that action had thereby caused others an immeasurable future of pain. I wanted an apology for that horrible legacy.

Dr. F says; *you must meet the person that was walking down the dock on the way to kill herself- and love her. That is forgiveness.* I contemplated this. I did feel great compassion for my mother. For all that, I can see that even forgiveness is not an endpoint. It is ongoing and exists in the midst of many contrasts: anger, compassion, pardon, mystery, peace, agitation, alcoholism, a good mother, and a beautiful human being who committed suicide. All of these things are part of the whole. The truth is all this and more existing at the same time.

Never had I been confronted so directly with the juxtapositions and stark contradictions in life: that there could be such unnaturalness in the face of such organic beauty; that we could all want so badly to live and, at the same time, so desperately to escape; that I could still find joy and laughter in the midst of this great pain. Through a force greater than me, I felt a bigger context to things, and I could now welcome it instead of just wondering at it. I felt the beauty and magnetism of this, and somehow it all made me feel more alive.

* * *

A GREATER PERSPECTIVE

Blame can be difficult to move through in grief because there may be someone who is directly at fault for the predicament of our loss. It can also be that we condemn other people in our lives who caused suffering to that person or to ourselves. Either way, our righteousness can become a barrier to moving forward. As long as we feel like a victim, we deprive ourselves of the opportunity to move through this painful experience in our lives with greater strength and autonomy. On a deep level, blame is simply a projection of our own deep sorrow. We think that if we find a culprit it will alleviate our suffering, but instead it only sows the seeds of bitterness.

In my case, indictment had come to be ingrained in my thoughts about my mother. I had carried close to me the ways in which she failed me, and had not taken the time to see her as a human being, whose only real failing was unconsciousness. She had not meant to cause all of the pain that she might have. She was only very, very human.

Where strong opinions and emotion come into play, we often allow ourselves insufficient space for everything to just be. Sometimes, just giving another person's opinion or strong emotion some room in our attention brings us closer to wisdom and acceptance in fraught matters of the heart. Allowing spaciousness between the stimulus and our response to it helps us access a middle ground. Acceptance of another does not mean agreement of opinion; it can simply be allowing territory for all of it.

The seventeenth gift of grief is that it opens the way to forgiveness. Sometimes when we mourn we are crying for everything we have ever lost. Grief brings up old wounds, and if we remain open, opportunities for forward momentum in seemingly intractable situations occur. Given space and openness, healing and closure are possible.

Ultimately, the antidote to a grudge is to give others what you would like to receive. Mercy in the face of unfairness, in the face of having been wronged, is one of the most powerfully transformative tools we can wield. When we give others our compassion, our acceptance, and our love, we receive the same gift in return in our lives many times over.

Forgiveness comes from a place of bounty. When we can feel the abundance in our own lives, in whatever form it takes, we recognize that bitterness is not worth it, as it only takes away from that feeling. When we are honest about our own human failings, it is easier to be humane toward another's. Then we realize that there is nothing to forgive, and we are able to turn once again to fully face and embrace the bounty of this life.

Space contemplation can be very helpful in helping us to remain open. Space gives us an absolute perspective. In it, we can hold a larger perspective of our relative unimportance, being just a tiny speck in an infinite universe, at the same time that we hold the pain of the world in our hearts. When we don't jump to fill in the expanse left by the loss, at the very least, grace can enter and bring the kind of solace that comes from it alone.

* * *

ANTIDOTE TO GRIEF
17. Forgiveness: An antidote to bitterness

FORGIVENESS CONTEMPLATION

Get comfortable and, if you wish, close your eyes. Shift your awareness to your breath, and breathe slowly and deeply. Breathe in relaxation and a sense of ease. Let go of any tension as you exhale. Let the warmth of relaxation flow through your whole body, from your head all the way down to your feet. Let your attention reach the still, quiet center of your being, with your body relaxed, your emotions calm, and your mind peaceful and spacious.

Become aware of the space in which all forms exist. Beneath everything there is only space, an infinite expanse. The body alone is comprised of 98% space and 2% matter. The universe is roughly the same. As you contemplate the larger space around and above you, experience the scale of yourself within this universe; a tiny speck on the earth, the earth a tiny speck in the galaxy, and all forms tiny specks in the vastness enfolding everything.

Remember a time when you experienced great wellbeing, enough to encompass mercy- perhaps when you were in a beautiful place or with a close friend. Bring an image of that moment to mind with as much detail as you can. Recollect what was happening; what the environment was like, if you were alone or with others, the accompanying sights and sounds. Specifically, remember what the experience of mercy felt like in your body- whether your body felt light, energetic, open, present, or clear. Continue to re-experience fully what forgiveness felt like in your body and mind. Let your awareness fully register this as you breathe in this sense of wellbeing. Relax into it with each exhalation.

Now move your awareness to your own individual form again, and the space inside your body. Notice the gap between your breaths, the opening between your thoughts, the space in which you sit, the reach between all movement, noise, and forms. This is the majority of the universe. This is the greater part of who you really are. Connect with the silent field of space that is the origin of all form. Bring this background into the foreground of your awareness.

Now, re-experiencing the feeling of mercy and wellbeing in your energy, imagine a slow inner smile beginning to spread in every cell of your body. As if every cell in your body could smile. Smile towards yourself and all that you are. Open toward life and all that you find there. Offer this welcome, this immense kindness towards all of it. Hold tenderness toward your pain, your intolerance, your sarcasm, and your discomfort. Imagine you are holding your own gentle hand in friendship. A smile holds space for compassion towards others and all that we encounter. In itself it is a kind of forgiveness. As you go through your day, continue to keep some of your awareness on the space in which the action of the day happens.

18

TRANSCENDENT ENDURANCE

The eyes are blind. One most look with the heart.
~Antoine St. Exupery

THE STORY

To tell a six year old that his grandmother did not find life worth living is rocking a very precious foundation indeed. I knew my son was curious about the event that he had lost a part of his mother's attention to over the past six months. I had discussed it with my therapist and had decided that when it came up, the truth, in whatever form was appropriate for a six-year-old boy, was the best course of action.

When I was putting him to bed one night in the spring, he honed in on me with his laser-like focus, and began asking all kinds of detailed questions about his grandmother's death. I wondered if it had come up recently, perhaps with one of his cousins. It felt like he knew that something about the story he had been told was left missing. So far, he had been told that his granny had died because of an accident that happened in her brain.

You are talking to Pops a lot. Going down to see him all the time, he said to me…Yes, I know, it's because of Granny. We are all pretty sad about it, and mad, I replied. *Why?* There are a lot of things about Granny's death that are hard, and when you are ready I can tell you about more about it… *I'm ready now. How did she die? Does it hurt when you die?*…Well, we can't really know because none of us remember dying and we haven't died yet in this life…*Does is it hurt if you get killed with a knife?*…Well, say for example someone did get killed with a knife. I think that probably the knife part would hurt. But I don't think it hurts when you leave your body.

You still didn't tell me about how Granny died... Well, Granny got sick in the mind... *What do you mean?* Well, you know how you can get sick in parts of your body? Sometimes you get sick in your mind, which means that your mind plays tricks on you–it can make you believe things that aren't true. *So how did she die?* Well, her mind got sick and she hurt herself. (He is flipped over, lying on his stomach.) *How?* Do you already know how (I am thinking he may have overheard something)? *No.* Well, it happened with a gun. *You mean like she turned it on herself and shotted herself?* Yes. (He is on his back now, hands over his eyes. He pauses.) *Where did she get the gun?* She bought it at a store. *Oh...*

...There are a few important things to know about this, I say. One is that what happened to Granny will never happen to us. *How do you know?* Because I am sure of it. I would never let my mind play tricks on me. *How can you not?* Well, it just wouldn't happen. Because I know that my mind is just a silly thing sometimes and not who I really am. So if it started to play tricks on me I would put it down for a nap. *Well, she's your mother so it will happen to you.* No, it won't, because when people get sick in the mind, there are doctors who can help make it better, and if my mind ever started to play tricks on me or tell me to do bad things, I would get help from a doctor or other people who love me. Also, I would never, ever touch or play with a gun because you know how I feel about guns or any kind of weapons that could hurt you.

Can you tell me the story about me being born, again? Sure I can. You'd like to talk about something happier, wouldn't you. *Yeah, this is sad.* Yes, it is. We're all sad about it. And I can tell you something else I know for certain. Do you remember the Granny that we knew, the one that was funny and played games with you and brought you candy and stuff? *Yeah.* Well, that is not the same part of Granny that did this. And I know that the wherever Granny is now, she is the same Granny that we knew and was so fun and stuff- her mind is not sick anymore and I know that she feels just as sorry and sad about what happened as we all do...

Now do you want me to tell you about the moment you were born? *Yeah.* Okay, but let me tell you one more important thing. You don't have to worry about that happening to me or Dad or any of us. *Yeah, I know, you've said that a few times now.* I know, but I want to make sure it gets in here, I say, jiggling his heart, and we laugh.

* * *

A GREATER PERSPECTIVE

Following any kind of loss comes steps we have to walk that require a great deal of forbearance. Attending a funeral, telling children or parents about the loss, dealing with secrets that are revealed after the death- these things can force us to expand our idea of what we thought we could handle in this life.

During these difficult moments on the road of grief, we are faced with taking action that can either strengthen or diminish us. Life is decided in these spaces, at these choice points, where clarity lies just behind the fog of our strong emotions. We may be tempted to skip the moment of opportunity, which comes in the form of brutal honesty. This is all so unrelenting, and we feel a sense of helplessness, or resignation, in the face of what is required of us. The inner fortitude that comes with grief assists us to turn tragedy into opportunity. Our courageous actions open the way for new patterns, new growth in ourselves and in those we love. My discussion with my son about his grandmother's suicide was my opportunity; what I said here made a difference. How I showed up would influence the moment when he, too, because of the legacy we had been left, might have to confront suicide as a reality in his own life.

I knew that he was asking for more detail than I would have thought was appropriate for a six-year-old child to hear. It was heartbreaking, and required a kind of inner resolution, to be the one to tell him that the world could be so uncertain, so perilous; and that the danger of violent destruction could exist within his own family. My instinct was to want to protect him from all of it. But I answered his questions because I recognized a kind of tenacity on the part of this young child, a demand for the truth. He could sense that there was more to the story than he was being told. Being honest with him at that moment felt like a message that, even though there were such tragic things in the world, there was also a stability in the way we withstood it; openly, honestly and with a determination to not let it rule our lives.

The eighteenth gift of grief is the establishment of transcendant endurance- a real deepening of patience with ourselves and others. We can access this by cradling ourselves in the awareness of a greater gentle, loving force both within us and surrounding us. This perspective leads us to acceptance of the deep loss we have experienced, strengthening us in endless ways. This inner fortitude, which we accept as a gift that comes with our loss, empowers us to deal with all sudden change in our lives. It also allows us to shine a stronger light for others who are struggling to gain this kind of inner resolution on their own journeys.

The knowledge that ultimately we are parented by a force more powerful, gentle and loving than even the best mother or father can lead to a deep, lasting sense of security in our experience. Like a benevolent guardian, it does not protect us from pain, but it does soften it. Parents, children, and families will come and go. We are transitory; but this gentle, ever-present, loving force is always there guiding us from our first moment in a body to our last. Tapping into this limitless supply of love, peace, and joy is like tapping into an endless source of fresh spring water. When we access it, we can share its gifts with others, benefiting everyone.

* * *

ANTIDOTE TO GRIEF
18. Nurturing Contemplation:
An antidote to resignation

NURTURING CONTEMPLATION: CRADLED IN AWARENESS

Become aware of the inner energy field of your body. Allow any thoughts to be there, but simply turn your greater attention toward the sensations in the body and the rhythm of the breath. Sit back comfortably and allow yourself to be blanketed in security by mother earth as if arms were wrapped around you, holding you securely. Now allow yourself to be cradled by your awareness, as if it is a soft cloud enveloping you in its tranquility. Cradle yourself in your own awareness, like a mother rocking her child. Your awareness, a part of this greater intelligence, this silent field of stillness, can support you, can hold everything. Allow this greater intelligence to nurture and cherish you, offering comfort, peace, and solace.

Feel the life giving energy at work in the body. Notice the health at work in it. Notice your heart. Become aware of the heart, and offer gratitude for its beating so relentlessly and consistently. Breathing in and out from the heart center, access a basic kindness toward yourself. Feel any areas of mental blockage or numbness, judgment, self-hatred. Then drop beneath that to the place where you find care for yourself, where you want strength and health and safety for yourself.

Allow yourself to be cradled in your own basic goodness as if you were an infant accepting love from its mother. Bask and nourish yourself in this energy of gentleness, peace, and acceptance. Invite images of love and solicitude to radiate into your whole being. Let this awareness, this tender care expand the heart and travel out into the room to others in your life, to the planet, and beyond.

Radiate kindness and peace to any image that comes into your mind. Allow the world to nourish itself from your tender attention to it. Now, as you breathe in, repeat Yes. Yes to life. As you breathe out, say thank you. Thank you to the earth, and to everything.

19

GRACE

Death is not the end, but is in itself a symbol of profound change, of transformation. Through being witness to someone's death we are offered the opportunity to go through our own profound transformation. Eventually we come to understand that it is transformation that is required of us, not misery.
~Robert Johnson

THE STORY

We have planned a summer memorial service for my mother in the spot in Maine where we spent all our summers growing up. Somehow it is like coming full circle. We are returning to the place where her descent started, where everything changed. It feels like I am on a rollercoaster, journeying toward the scene of her death. I know what happens, and I would like to get off, but the ride just keeps going.

Last summer in Maine was not only the major marking of the end of her life, but the reliving of the beginning of the tragedy that brought it about. I remember an awful helplessness as everything began to take on a momentum of its own. My mother was in a terrible place. I knew that something was very wrong with her. She seemed to have lost all vehemence for anything.

I remember being at the architect's office in an endless meeting about the new house our family was building. We were huddled at a table in the basement for hours, going over details like the pitch of the roof, copper vs. pvc valleys, what types of risers to use for the staircase, and where we wanted each electrical outlet. The engineering architect had a fifteen-minute answer to every question. I kept looking over at my mother, wondering why I felt no tension coming from her direction. Why she wasn't pacing like a caged lion, like she usually did at having to sit for more than half an hour? Why wasn't she sighing and rolling her eyes at these pointless details, clutching her purse in her lap and practically popping out of her seat because it was way past time to leave and yet we all had to sit and wait for some extra thing like a copy of the lighting plan or the thing we just bought making its way out from the storage room out back or someone checking to see if they had the color we wanted or the long overdue check at a restaurant?

The memory of her extreme detachment makes me wince. Especially when I recall that, sometime during this summer, in discussing her state with my brother-in-law, I now remember saying carelessly that it was like *she had lost her will to live* or something, like the only thing keeping her alive was her fear of death. It did not occur to me consciously to consider how much pain she must have been in. She had learned to hide that so well from her daughters- she had spent a lifetime cultivating an expertise in managing emotions through secret measures- that I had stopped asking these questions of my all too human mother.

As I remember these things, I want to speak with her more than anything. I am re-watching this movie. I have seen what happens next, and this is my one last chance to save her. Now I know what would say and what I would change about my behavior to try and alter things. The morning of her memorial service, I go down to the rocks on the beach in front of her house. The sky is wide and all absorbing, and as I sit I talk to her up there:

Hey Mom. I am watching this movie of my life with you, from the beginning. I know how it ends, so the movie has this new perspective, this new depth. Before, I couldn't properly characterize the earlier parts. Their full context is only apparent now. I am approaching the finale of the film, reliving it all over again, only as I watch I want to run into the screen and scream, Wait!! Let's go back and change the future. Isn't there anything I could do to change the end? I wanted so badly for your breakdown to be- as I had expected it would be- your redemption, not your undoing.

In the movie you provide us with redemption, but in such an awful way. And when I watch it, I stop so many times at myself and the things I said and did which I would take back. I want to play the character of me only better this time, as I am today. I'd like to cut the part where I snap at you while we are taking the Christmas card picture in the garden last summer. That was so insensitive. You were so helpless, and so down. I'd have a lot more compassion for you during that last summer. You were so separate, and so desperate. I wouldn't be so annoyed with you for being human. I would sit down and tell you how worried I was about you, and how much I cared. I'd stay with you and guide you through your dark time. I'd tell you about watching your thoughts and help you watch your pain and be your witness for it.

Then I'd cut the part where I kept my anxiety and worry about you at bay all fall, downplaying your illness because I couldn't face its serious- ness. I'd cut the part where I spouted professional wisdom, at you, at Julia and Miranda, and at Dad. I'd listen to that awful feeling I had in my stomach the day in September you told me that the doctor had prescribed for you, of all things, Prozac, and I'd call him right away and question his decision. I'd remind him of your negative family history with Prozac. I'd tell him you were an active alcoholic. I'd be more active in finding a psy- chiatrist sooner. I'd edit the part where I feel a kind of vindication in your depression (because it is proof that what goes around comes around- that bottled up feelings eventually come out for all of us- we can't escape them, that no one is immune from universal justice, and this is your redemption).

Here are all the things I wish I had said to you: I love you. You're a fool. You can't leave us. We need you. Snap out of it. Stop drinking. Go to rehab again; get some therapy. This is dangerous; you've sunk dan- gerously low. Let us help you. This has no ultimate power other than what you give it. It is temporary; you will come out of it. Stop believing in it. Trust us. It's not worth it. Don't you see how out of perspective things have gotten. Look clearly. It's not worth dying over. Dying can't be the only way out of this. That's the suffering talking. The power you're giving it is absurd. Its not as big as you think it is. You have everything to live for. It's all up to you and it's a new way for you. Love yourself. Don't talk yourself into doing something stupid. Don't talk yourself out of something smart. I can feel that you are giving up. Find a way to come back. It's not all up to you. You don't control everything in the world. There are other benevolent forces, and help in others.

But I can't do or say any of these things. I can't change what happened. I can only watch as it draws closer. Mom, I hope you can forgive me for all of the ways in which I hurt you or contributed to your pain. I forgive you everything.

As I walk up to the church for the memorial service, I feel cleaner, and I am able to speak in depth about my mother to this group of people who loved her so well all her life, and who are suffering with this loss as well.

EULOGY FROM THE MEMORIAL SERVICE FOR MY MOTHER:

I think it would be difficult for me to talk about mom without first touching on how she died, because it is certainly something that has flooded all of our thinking about her over the last months. I've always been a person of great hope and yet it is hard to feel optimism about anything when the possibility exists that things could end in suicide. I have felt every emotion- worry, guilt, anger, and obsession- in trying to make sense of this. I've tried out every possible explanation for it.

And in the end, I have found that no one paradigm or story could ever perfectly fit this or any other picture of life and death. Nor can it remove my pain about it. There are some mysteries that are larger than the human mind. Mom's truth as she experienced it will never be fully known to us, and we are all left with the simple, sad fact that she was so loved and now she is gone from us. For my part I am left with few certainties about the world. However, those that remain I'd like to share with you.

First, I know a few things for certain about mom and the kind of effect she had on our family. She was a bright, bold, dramatic centerpiece that infused joy and humor into our experience. She taught us to be down to earth, independent, opinionated, appreciative of the beautiful, and always maintain our sense of humor. It is to her credit that as a family we found ourselves able to laugh within days of the sudden and terrible fact of her death. She had a brilliant, wickedly bizarre wit which made the ordinary in life seem extra-ordinary and the heavy things seem simply absurd.

As a mother she was creative and fun- she had the most original games, surprises, parties- anything to reinforce the idea that life was an adventure. A rainy afternoon in Wisconsin turned into a full blown adult production of Cinderella for us, with mom starring as Prince Charming; a car ride to Maine was really a chance to go on tour with our air band- tennis rackets serving as microphones, guitars, and drums; making dinner turned into a pasta party with homemade spaghetti drying on broomsticks and chairs all over the house and half of the town gathering to eat it.

As we grew, she loved us fiercely and protectively. She bragged of each accomplishment to anyone who would listen. Things that went wrong or gave us trouble were never our fault. When we were younger, before our summer cottage had a foundation put in, there was a dark, mildewy ex- panse of space under the living room floor where all kinds of porcupines, chipmunks, wasps, and things lived. Fights with friends, boyfriends, prob- lems with teachers, illicit parties- these things were always someone else's fault, and mom's imaginary punishment for them was simple- fling them under the house and make them live there until they came to their senses.

Another certainty that remains for me is that once they came along, there were 8 things that gave my mother her greatest joy- her grandchil- dren. As a grandmother, she was creative and enthusiastic- whether it be in her providing the perfect jello treat or Archie comic for them, hosting sleepovers, or taking a carload of kids to the pool. She prided herself on having both the most and the most brilliant grandchildren (and rightfully so, too). Her last words to each of us daughters centered around them.

And despite the fact that she was little able to form words or speak at all at that point, she still wanted to know every current detail about them.

To say we all miss her is an understatement. The centerboard was taken out of our ship and we have all been trying to right her again. So many times I have found myself thinking, "Mom would have loved that"- a deep suntan, a brilliant color, a good gossip, Belgian shoes, a trip on the whaler to Bar Harbor for ice cream and a peek in the rock shop, a promising house snoop, fresh lemon, camellias, lilacs, the dogwood tree behind the house in full bloom, and any and every tiny thing that her grandchildren did.

Her love of them was not misplaced. Watching all of my family these last months- their courage and grace- (Dad, Julia, Miranda, Jay- and all of the kids and brother-in-laws)- has been awe-inspiring. What is at the heart of each of them is so brilliant, so amazing that it takes my breath away. Through them I've seen that pain can overcome all of us, but we can also overcome pain. Life is a gift we honor by living. And any time we feel anything less than that, we only need to reach out for help until it passes and we are in our right mind again.

I picture mom in a tranquil place now, and I know that she was greeted with the ultimate peace- the peace that passes all understanding- the moment she left consciousness. What a great surprise for one who felt so unexpecting of it in her life and so unworthy of it at the time of her death.

And in life, I am left with a happy image of her, too, up here in her summer home. She is at the pool, sitting in a beach chair, face to the sun. There is the lively noise of children playing and splashing around her, and every once in awhile one runs up to her to whisper something or give her a poke, or get a piece of candy from the pocket of her shorts. She is chatting about this or that (some of which is gossip), surrounded by friends and family, who are all smiling or laughing at something she has just said.

* * *

A GREATER PERSPECTIVE

Working with grief is a sticky process. There are many ways to become trapped along the way. Self-contempt, or antipathy toward anything or anyone, can be one of the ways we become stuck in a particular phase of grief.

Contempt is another form of anger. When we feel this persisting, we can ask ourselves: years from now, how do we want to remember this loss and our choices and behavior in the face of it? Do we want the memory of this loved one to be associated with acrimony? Moving forward, would they want us to be filled with self-contempt? What feelings are unresolved for us as a result of this loss? The answers to these questions will help us gain new perspective in places where we feel ensnared and guide us toward grace. Getting stuck in contempt is avoided by continuing to ask ourselves how we want this experience to be incorporated.

What Mark Epstein writes about spirituality and Buddhism applied to psychotherapy in his book, Thoughts Without a Thinker, can be applied to directly to grief. In it, he says that *the progression from distance to connection is the essence of the spiritual path...the journey is at times excruciating and at others exhilarating, and all along the way there is our consistent, dedicated attention anchoring it all.* [11] With our attention, we walk the tightrope between pain and suffering, and we find a new dimension of life awaiting us, gentle and tranquil.

Tolerance and composure are the rewards we find when we wake up to ourselves and our circumstances. The composure that comes with forbearance and steadfastness helps us move more fluidly through grief. **The nineteenth gift of grief is grace.** Grace enters when we accept the things we cannot change about our loss. Grace requires alertness: instants of grace are moments of space which we are able to fully inhabit.

Stability contemplation can help us access grace. The mountain is steadfast. Its solidity exemplifies accepting whatever comes our way in life. In its consistency lies its grace.

* * *

ANTIDOTE TO GRIEF
19. Stability contemplation:
An antidote for contempt

STABILITY CONTEMPLATION: THE MOUNTAIN

Imagine a giant mountain. You are the mountain. Your thoughts- most of the action of life- is happening on the surface of the mountain. The weather of life- strong winds, rain, sleet, ice, snow- deep emotions and ups and downs- happens at the surface of the mountain. Sometimes the weather is uplifting- with warm sunshine and clear skies, the growth of new life and possibility. Other times it is so raw it is physically painful. Throughout all of this, there is another part of the mountain that remains, deep, still, and unchanging. Place your attention on the quiet place of stillness at the center of the mountain. As you watch the weather of life shift, keep the majority of your attention in this field of stillness at the center of your being.

Whatever the weather of life is, there is always a deeper part of you at your core that remains centered and constant. Like all forms, the mountain is changing, but your awareness, the watcher, the space between the form and the formless, is the constant. It gives your life context and constancy. By anchoring yourself in solidity, you can face whatever weather comes your way with grace.

20

WISDOM

Where there is love there are always great miracles.
~ Willa Cather

~

...The window you have been looking through continues to shimmer and sparkle but the images are receding now, and you can no longer get a clear view of anything at all. It has become a reflection of the outside world itself- a world of sun and water, trees and sky- an immense expanse of endless openness, infinite and immeasurable, completely unfathomable.

You are reluctant to turn toward to dock again but you hear something coming from that direction, almost like the sound of a bell. After a few moments you realize that it is the laughter of children. As your gaze follows it you see several children running down the long dock in the bright morning sunshine- their hands are lifted in the air as they shout with joy, in a race for the boathouse and the sea treasures at the end of the pier. Several blond women follow behind. Their steps are light and you sense a deep joy emanating from them and all of the surroundings...

THE STORY

At the year anniversary of her death, my father and sisters and I meet in Virginia again. Our visits here have become sparser and more sporadic. Life is beginning its forward momentum once again. The past has been put down to rest, for now. The presence feels less foreign, and as always, the future calls out to us through dreams and desires. There is more life than death in my existence once more. I have reached a place where life has begun to dance again, and I can feel an ever-deepening connection to the world around me.

As we always do, we walk the labyrinth together in silence, down the shore from where my mother took her last breath. Back at the house, we pace to the end of the long dock together, to the boathouse. Each time I walk to the end of this dock I think, *Every step was a choice she made.* One hundred and ten steps. Yet I know now that her mind could not see anything in these moments but escape.

Enlightenment is love expressed in every moment, all kinds of love. If suicide is self-hatred, then the antidote is self-love. My mother's suicide left more room for that in our family. In the months after her death, a number of my extended family achieved sobriety. My youngest sister and father had a mutually agreed upon visit and achieved a kind of tentative accord. And together, my two other sisters, my father and I began to relate to one another with an amazing amount of love and understanding between us.

This was a new thing. I knew that all of us, including my mother, had always had great love for one another, but it had often sat under the surface of our family, unexpressed. Strong emotion spilled out through uncontrolled bouts of crying or nervous laughter. Now, for the first time, we felt free to express love. We actually felt a necessity about it, and we received the immediate effects of it.

When I contemplated this, I saw an immensely complex web, like the one I felt during the full moon eclipse on the night of her death. Things made sense in such a many layered way- the generations of alcoholism and repression freed, the effects of the sexual abuse lightened. It felt like she liberated us from this heavy family lineage, a mantle that we were all unconsciously carrying. I can think of some better ways this might have come about, but still I felt it as a success of sorts of hers. On the surface, her final act made her life appear to be such a failure. However, I could feel a peculiar universal sense in it. I would never completely understand the deed itself, but I could certainly see clearly the positive effects springing from it.

The boathouse looks the same. There are still the subtle dark stains where we tried to wash her away. Part of me wants to sit in the corner where she did it again, but I suddenly realize, *what's the point?* I will never understand what she did. It will always be a mystery to me.

We spread her ashes in the water. There are crumbly bits of bone in the soft dust. *That was her body once,* I think. We sit in silence at the end of the dock, enfolded by the fluidity of the afternoon fall light. Somehow, the surroundings seem even more beautiful in contrast to the event. The warm sun shines brilliant on the water. I can hear the call of birds in the whispering trees on the shore. There is a feathery breeze and the water laps gently against the pier. The intensity of this moment envelops us, humming with aliveness. It could not be any fuller or more complete.

My family and I have completed a journey of sorts. We allowed ourselves to fall into the canyon of death, hoping we would find our way back out again. We underwent a kind of family reckoning. At times we had all wondered if we would ever return to any sense of connection with the greater world.

But there is no end point to grief; there are just way stations along the road. We have moved beyond the place where life meets death, moved past the sky at the visible atmosphere, to see the immensity of the other side. Now we are able to embrace life more strongly than before, and I somehow feel grateful to my mother for this experience.

As I sit at the end of the pier, I feel like a piece of some larger galactic puzzle, only the tiniest part of which I understand. I have a sense that everything is going according to plan; that there is some greater sense in this. I can see the future and the past melded together in this infinity of the present moment. I see years of activity in this place: dusk and light, shadow and sun, turbulence and tranquility. I see darkness and pain, the fury of storms- snow and ice- and the silent field of stillness so apparent at the end of one. I hear feet on the dock: children are running down it, laughing with joy and looking for crabs in the traps. I see people sitting in harmony in the corner of the boathouse, absorbing the incredible peace reaching out to us in every moment.

* * *

A GREATER PERSPECTIVE

It has occurred to me more than once in this life how close a nervous breakdown is to a spiritual breakthrough. In both cases, all of our conditioning comes apart and nothing familiar remains. As Deb Shapiro says in Your Body Speaks Your Mind, *you can turn a breakdown into a breakthrough by trusting yourself and keeping people close by who can help you.*[12] In my family's case, the breakdown of our life as we knew it became a breakthrough for us. In my mother's case it did not.

It rings very true to me now the primary goal of suicide is not to end life but to end pain. I know that my mother was searching for self-love. The act, her murdering herself, may have been an extreme act of violence and hatred, but what she was reaching for in the act was love.

If self-immolation is the ultimate expression of self-hatred, then the only antidote to it is to love oneself unconditionally. This seems to me to be the remedy for any kind of suffering. Not the kind of love that leaves out the shadow, the unconscious, but the kind of love where you've seen it all, the very best and the very worst of you, and you love yourself anyway. You welcome all parts of life. What a soft, appealing way of being.

There is a choice as we go through the intense mourning period of grief. We could choose not to look toward the pain of our loss. We could choose to control or suppress it. Ultimately, we have the right through free will to choose wrong, make mistakes, misjudge, act a fool, be insane, and to commit murder. To choose when we exit is an extension of this free will. It is up to us to discern whether this represents freedom or not. I do know that what feels better when we experience it, what feels more authentic, is wisdom. True liberation is not liberation from life but it is liberation to live life more fully.

The greatest gift of grief is, ultimately, the wisdom that it brings. This wisdom is the joy that we allow ourselves to embrace mixed with the humility that comes from recognizing life's fragility through having experienced it firsthand. That we would be humble in the face of something so awesome as birth or death and their accompanying mysteries seems right somehow. It shows reverence for something greater than our human understanding.

Wisdom comes out of the darkness. We have experienced a great chasm, and a richness is added to life because of the contrast our suffering has provided between how it is and how we would like it to be. Hand in hand with this comes a deepening of joy for what we have been through, and a respect for our newfound substance. Eventually, enthusiasm for life returns with more vigor for what we have lost.

To be fully engaged and connected to someone and be comfortable with the full realization that they could disappear at any moment- leave you, die, commit suicide; to understand directly that all of these possibilities/realities exist at the same time, is wisdom. Unity meditation helps us to access the wisdom we have gained. It is the antidote to ignorance. It is the antidote to all grief. To stay connected with all life, unified with the entire universe, is the solution to everything.

* * *

ANTIDOTE TO GRIEF
20. Unity contemplation: An antidote to ignorance

UNITY CONTEMPLATION

Become aware of the breath. Place your full attention on each aspect of it. Notice the inhale and the exhale, as well as the pauses in the breath. Notice the larger cycle of the breath, and the space in which it happens. Feel the lifegiving quality of it. Now become aware of the many billions of breathing cycles taking place in this moment- of people, animals, and all living beings. You are connected to all of it through the breath. As you join with and experience this symphony, begin to sync the breath with the larger breathing cycles in nature; the trees and plants, the seasons, the oceans and tides. Now allow your breath to move with the greater flow of the larger planetary movements in our solar system and beyond, all moving to-gether in concert. You are the space, connected to all of this. You are one with everything, and you are magnificent.

CONCLUSION

Nothing is worth more than this day.
~ Goethe

I am always struck by the notion taught in many traditions of meditation that pain is a feeling of awake. Maybe that's why we are so drawn to violence on television and in the media. We are ashamed at the things we are impelled to watch sometimes, or the links we push on the internet, or the violent news videos we can't seem to help but be taken in by. Maybe this is because it wakes a part of us up, a part of us that is deeply connected to the rest of humanity. We all feel deep pain in this life, and we want to know how other people get through it. I think we also feel a deep desire to connect with others, and this is one of the few ways we are being offered to do it.

Grief wakes us up. If we get stuck along the way, if we fall back asleep, then we need outside forces to sound the alarm and arouse us. If we continue to move through it with courage and consideration, then we mine the treasure that is revealed to us during it. We carry it with us into the rest of our lives, and spread it around wherever we go, making the entire world a richer place.

The gems that we now have access to allow us to continue to awaken and feel fully engaged in life. We don't need to imagine the worst possible scenario, or see it, to feel more alive. We don't need to adhere to the extreme alternatives of attachment or aversion in life. We can find a way of being, a delicate balance, which is in harmony with the transience of the world without being oppressed by it. We can awaken into the sacredness of our own pain and use it as a basis for compassion toward others. We don't need to bond over the miseries in our lives to the extent that it creates an atmosphere of more negativity. When we know that connection lies in not getting stuck, not stopping anywhere, we can keep moving together in the present, at the same time creating a more positive place in the future.

Grief is a mystical journey, and any such exploration is formidable. It requires faith and hope. Faith that, even though we cannot see it, there is some larger purpose to what life hands us. And hope that we will eventually feel fully alive again. It is our job, while grieving or on any journey, to make the most of our precious time here. In this world, which on the surface encompasses ignorance, unconsciousness, and disparagement of self and other, it is up to us to look more deeply to find the joy and the engagement in the amazing, magnetic, enthralling, and fascinating thing called life.

Death causes us to ask the big questions. When he heard about my mother's death, my six-year-old son verbalized this perfectly when he asked me, "*Where did she go?*". As we ponder questions like this, it is important to remember to be gentle with ourselves: not knowing everything is perfectly okay. In fact, it is fine and even extremely beneficial to get comfortable with the unanswerable. When we become more intimate with these enigmas, we transcend life and death into a realm of experience both boundless and eternal.

There is no end to the grieving process. Like life, the nature of our grief is constantly changing. The gifts of grief are most obviously available to us, the openings are the largest, during the period of intense mourning, but because of what we have been through, we will never lose our access to the treasure that comes with great loss.

The ultimate answer to any grief is to grab the joy and live it again. Turning away from certain occasions, even the difficult ones, keeps us from fully experiencing life. Remembering to touch each moment as it goes by is the antidote to the kind of disconnection that is so common at this time in our technologically advanced history. This is suicide prevention as well. This is the absolute counteragent to loss of any kind, be it accident, murder, suicide, divorce, catastrophe, or old age.

The greatest value of grief is that through it, we are transformed. To a certain degree, through our reactions and our behavior, we get to decide how. The more awake we remain during the process, the more curious than afraid we attempt to be, the greater the riches we will find. As we transcend the suffering, as we recognize our self as made up of more than just what happens to us, we can experience new heights of empathy, endurance, mercy, kindness, fortitude, humility, compassion, insight, grace, wisdom, and all the very best of what it means to be human and alive.

the end

10 WAYS TO HONOR GRIEF:

1. **Surrender.** Using the path of least resistance, go with the flow of the river. It is either going to control you or you are going to control it. Clarity comes with acceptance, fog with resistance.

2. **Let go of how it used to be.** Move beyond your story, and you will find an expanded version of yourself.

3. **It's okay to feel bad.** Allow the turbulent emotions. Remember the difference between pain & suffering. Pain is what happens. Suffering is what your reaction to the pain. Move beyond the personal. Don't mistake your suffering for who you are.

4. **Have compassion: be kind to yourself.** Exercise, eat well, be a gentle friend to yourself.

5. **As you encounter space, embrace the new unknown for a while.** Grace can only enter when you leave space for it. This space is where you percolate on and envision your new story. Find the universal in the experience and connect to it: you are not alone. There are millions of people on the planet who have experienced loss and the accompanying gap left behind.

6. **Find the gold in the space.** Find the gem that is hidden in every tragedy. What is your personal lesson? Look for the silver lining. Look for another way to view the situation than the one you feel stuck in.

7. **Become comfortable with uncertainty.** Find stability in the constancy of life's instability. Connect with nature. Find faith in the mountain's ability to sustain itself even during the strongest storm.

8. **Recreate your reality.** Decide your perspective on the event. Your perception of and interpretation of the situation is determining your current reality.

9. **Practice gratitude.** Embrace new possibilities and the pure potentiality of this new situation. Something great is going to happen today.

10. **Practice Forgiveness.** Give what you want to receive.

THE GIFTS OF GRIEF:

1. Grief brings the blessing of shock, where our mind is quieted and our body is calm.

2. Grief provides moments of intense clarity and spiritual wonder by connecting us to the present moment.

3. Grief connects us with something greater than our own mind: nature, which can gently hold the enormity of what we feel.

4. Grief bonds us to the best of humanity by giving us access to deep human connection, goodwill, kindness, and love.

5. Grief is accompanied by a sense of separation from our story, which allows us to experience our sense of who we are in new and expanded ways.

6. Grief gives us more direct access to the deep well of peace and stillness around and inside us, helping to manage strong emotions.

7. Grief brings with it an instant deepening in connection with loved ones, which can help heal old emotional wounds.

8. Grief puts us in touch with the greater mystery of birth and death.

9. Grief offers us the opportunity to become aware of and give way to the flow of life.

10. Grief exposes us to impressions of forces greater than ourselves at work in the universe.

11. Grief brings a sense of connection to and comfort in being alive, in all life.

12. Grief reconnects us to gratitude for the gift of life.

13. Grief brings true compassion, a sense of deep connection and empathy with all living, suffering beings.

14. Grief helps us step outside of time and into the present moment, where all life is happening.

15. Grief broadens our frame of reference on life, teaching us flexibility.

16. Grief brings perspective and clarity.

17. Grief opens the way to forgiveness of all kinds.

18. Grief creates transcendent endurance- a real deepening of patience with ourselves and others.

19. Grief brings grace.

20. Grief brings wisdom- and a deepening of joy for what we have been through for having felt the contrast.

ANTIDOTES TO GRIEF:

Contemplations for
Mining the Treasure Inherent in Great Loss

1. **INNER BODY CONTEMPLATION:**
An antidote to sudden trauma/shock

2. **ALLOWING CONTEMPLATION:**
An antidote to resistance/disbelief

3. **NATURE CONTEMPLATION:**
An antidote to feeling overwhelmed

4: **WALKING CONTEMPLATION:**
An antidote to a sense of devastation

5. **WITNESS CONTEMPLATION:**
An antidote to a sense of denial

6. **STILLNESS CONTEMPLATION:**
An antidote to remorse

7. **SILENCE CONTEMPLATION:**
An antidote to stark emotional anguish

8. **OPEN SKY CONTEMPLATION:**
An antidote to intellectualization

9. **FLOW OF LIFE CONTEMPLATION:**
An antidote to control

10. **SURRENDER CONTEMPLATION:**
An antidote to bargaining

11. **HEARTBEAT CONTEMPLATION:**
An antidote to desolation

12. <u>GRATITUDE OF LIFE CONTEMPLATION</u>:
An antidote to isolation

13. <u>BREATH OF LIFE CONTEMPLATION</u>:
An antidote to oversensitivity

14. <u>PRESENT MOMENT CONTEMPLATION</u>:
An antidote to disorientation

15. <u>FLEXIBILITY CONTEMPLATION</u>:
An antidote to resistance

16. <u>PAIN CONTEMPLATION</u>: An antidote to anger

17. <u>FORGIVENESS CONTEMPLATION</u>:
An antidote to bitterness

18. <u>NURTURING CONTEMPLATION</u>:
An antidote to resignation

19. <u>STABILITY CONTEMPLATION</u>:
An antidote to contempt

20. <u>UNITY CONTEMPLATION</u>:
An antidote to ignorance

APPENDIX IV

10 common characteristics of completed suicides

1. <u>The common purpose of suicide is to seek a solution.</u>

Suicide is not a pointless or random act. To people who think about ending their own lives, suicide represents an answer to an otherwise insoluble problem or a way out of some unbearable dilemma. It is a choice that is somehow preferable to another set of dreaded circumstances, emotional distress, or disability, which the person fears more than death. Attraction to suicide as a potential solution may be increased by a family history of similar behavior. If someone else whom the person admired or cared for has committed suicide, then the person is more likely to do so.

2. <u>The common goal of suicide is cessation of consciousness.</u> People who commit suicide seek the end of the conscious experience, which to them has become an endless stream of distressing thoughts with which they are preoccupied. Suicide offers oblivion.

3. <u>The common stimulus (or information input) in suicide is intolerable psychological pain.</u> Excruciating negative emotions - including shame, guilt, anger, fear, and sadness - frequently serve as the foundation for self-destructive behavior. These emotions may arise from any number of sources.

4. <u>The common stressor in suicide is frustrated psychological needs.</u> People with high standards and expectations are especially vulnerable to ideas of suicide when progress toward these goals is suddenly frustrated. People who attribute failure or disappointment to their own shortcomings may come to view themselves as worthless, incompetent or unlovable. Family turmoil is an especially important source of frustration to adolescents. Occupational and interpersonal difficulties frequently

precipitate suicide among adults. For example, rates of suicide increase during periods of high unemployment (Yang et al., 1992).

5. The common emotion in suicide is hopelessness-helplessness. A pervasive sense of hopelessness, defined in terms of pessimistic expectations about the future, is even more important than other forms of negative emotion, such as anger and depression, in predicting suicidal behavior (Weishaar & Beck, 1992). The suicidal person is convinced that absolutely nothing can be done to improve his or her situation; no one else can help.

6. The common internal attitude in suicide is ambivalence. Most people who contemplate suicide, including those who eventually kill themselves, have ambivalent feelings about this decision. They are sincere in their desire to die, but they simultaneously wish that they could find another way out of their dilemma.

7. The common cognitive state in suicide is constriction. Suicidal thoughts and plans are frequently associated with a rigid and narrow pattern of cognitive activity that is comparable to tunnel vision. The suicidal person is temporarily unable or unwilling to engage in effective problem-solving behaviors and may see his or her options in extreme, all or nothing terms. As Shneidman points out, slogans such as "death before dishonor" may have a certain emotional appeal, but they do not provide a sensible basis for making decisions about how to lead your life.

8. The common action in suicide is escape. Suicide provides a definitive way to escape from intolerable circumstances, which include painful self-awareness (Baumeister, 1990).

9. The common interpersonal act in suicide is communication of intention. One of the most harmful myths about suicide is

the notion that people who really want to kill themselves don't talk about it. Most people who commit suicide have told other people about their plans. Many have made previous suicidal gestures. Schneidman estimates that in at least 80 percent of completed suicides, the people provide verbal or behavioral clues that indicate clearly their lethal intentions.

10. <u>The common consistency in suicide is with life-long coping patterns.</u> During the crisis that precipitate suicidal thoughts, people generally employ the same response patterns that they have used throughout their lives. For example, people who have refused to ask for help in the past are likely to persist in that pattern, increasing their sense of isolation.

http://www.survivorsofsuicide.com/understanding.shtml

Preventing Suicide:
Adapted from Marsha Linehan's
Reasons for Living Inventory:

STATEMENTS TO CONSIDER:

* I have a responsibility and commitment to my family.

* I believe I can learn to adjust to, or cope with, my problems.

* I believe I have control over my life and destiny.

* I believe only God has the right to end a life.

* I am afraid of death.

* I want to watch my children as they grow.

* Life is all we have and is better than nothing.

* I have future plans I am looking forward to carrying out.

* No matter how bad I feel, I know that it will not last.

* I love and enjoy my family too much and could not leave them.

* I am afraid that my method of killing myself would fail.

* I was to experience all that life has to offer, and there are many experiences I have not had yet that I want to have.

* It would not be fair to leave the children for others to take care of.

* I have a love of life.

* I am too stable to kill myself.

* My religious beliefs forbid it.

* The effect on my children could be harmful.

* It would hurt my family too much and I would not want them to suffer.

* I am concerned about what others would think of me.

* I consider it morally wrong.

* I still have many things left to do.

* I have the courage to face life.

* I am afraid of the actual "act" of killing myself (the pain, blood, violence)

* I believe killing myself would not really accomplish or solve anything.

* Other people would think I am weak and selfish.

* I would not want people to think I did not have control over my life.

* I would not want my family to feel guilty afterward.

APPENDIX VII

Email from my Mother in India,
written one year before her suicide

From: Barbara Hunt

Date: Tue Jan 21, 2003 11:36:28 AM US/Eastern

To: Miranda Hunt Borden, Leslie Hunt Palumbo, Julia Hunt Bogardus

Subject: INDIA!!!

In a message dated 1/21/2003 6:00:15 AM Eastern Standard Time: Barbara Hunt writes:

I have been very frustrated trying to get online, and have been helped by two patient Indians, who mutter "Hotmail, Hotmail" and then tell me I don't exist. But we have politely, very politely, with much bowing and nodding, established that I can write you, and will you forward to Miwa and Leslie as their email addresses aren't as clear to me as yours. WELL!! We are at the glorious Lake Palace Hotel in Udaipur, and have come to know our group well. I will tell you my highlights first in case this machine decides to whisk me away before I finish. We had, the second day of the trip, when we were still somewhat jet-lagged, a rickshaw ride. There were two to a rickshaw, pulled by a tiny fellow on a bicycle, through the streets of Old Delhi, with the alleys getting increasingly narrow until the buildings nearly met over our heads, two way traffic with BARELY enough room for the three wheeled rickshaw, who got their wheels tangled several times, and through it all the insistent mo-peds passed us and when they couldn't BEEPED and BEEPED. There were people by the sides of the narrow alleys selling all kinds of food, practically in the path of our bike, and in tiny stores no bigger than your downstairs bathroom, piled one next to the other cheek-by-jowel the most beautiful sari silks, all hung so gracefully and flowers and jewelry and trinkets, and people begging and yelling, and on and on we sped, clinging to the rickety vehicle for about 40 minutes, with all the sights, sounds and smells exploding around us. I have never seen anything like it, and when we finished we were speechless.

We did a lot of driving on the bus through Old Delhi, New Delhi and Agra or any other city we were in. I think on our first trip with the S's they tried to keep us away from scenes that might trouble us, but not this bunch. We have seen it all, including a meat market, not a pretty sight. I will jump into the next paragraph rather than trying to do it properly, because I feel this machine is waiting, waiting for me to try something smart so it can erase all my efforts and send me to purdah. The other highlight for me was the town of Jodhpur. We have books on it, and I have seen pictures but could not believe that a town/fort/palace could actually be like that. It is unbelievable--the town nestles at the foot of the fort. A great many houses are painted a lavender-blue, which looks like hydrangea blue in the shadows, and then the fort rises out of sheer rock 400 feet into the air. Kind of like the Masada must have. You wind up hairpin switchbacks until the bus can go no further. Then you walk, through HUGE gates, upon some of which are the hennaed handprints of the many little Ranis who were on their way to fling themselves on their husbands' funeral pyres.

When you get to the top, up on the battlements you are on top of the world. There is a palace up there, with luxe rooms and stained glass. All the way up and down you are followed and plucked at and yelled at by insistent hawkers of junk. You ignore them absolutely, but they persist. We got used to it. We have seen some fantastic Hindu temples, also Jain, but nothing quite so dramatic as with the S's in South India at night, when you REALLY THOUGHT that the God Shiva, or whoever, was actually going to step out of the litter in which he was supposedly being carried. But dramatic and elaborate and beautiful anyway.

We have, knock on wood, been healthy and careful while enjoying WONDERFUL food and spicy pickles etc. Accommodations are mostly good, sometimes great, and we spent 2 nights in tents in the desert, albeit deluxe tents with lanterns, carpets, running cold water, and wonderful sounds in the night like Hindu chanting from the temples, and drumming. I will now attempt to send this, and pray to Vishnu or Devi to not lose or erase it. Back

next Tuesday late. the 27th. XOX to all Grannie

Footnotes

[1]. Shapiro, Deb. Your Body Speaks your Mind. Boulder, Colorado. Sounds True Publishing, Inc., 2006. p. 328

[2]. Lewis, C.S. A Grief Observed. New York, New York. Harper Collins, 1961.

[3]. Halifax, Joan. The Fruitful Darkness. New York, New York. Grove Press, 1993. p. 49

[4]. Breggin, Peter R. Talking Back to Prozac: What Doctors Aren't Telling you About Today's Most Controversial Drug. New York, New York. St. Martin's Press,1994.

[5]. www.suicidology.org

[6]. www.suicidology.org

[7]. Hillman, James. Suicide and the Soul. New York, New York. Harper and Row, 1998. P. 121

[8]. Dalai Lama. The Tibetan Book of the Dead: The Great Book of Natural Liberation Through Understanding in the Between. New York, New York. Penguin Group, 2006. p. 4

[9]. Dalai Lama. The Tibetan Book of the Dead: The Great Book of Natural Liberation Through Understanding in the Between. New York, New York. Penguin Group, 2006. *xxi*

[10]. Chodron, Pema. When Things Fall Apart. Boston, Massachusetts. Shambala Publications,1997. p. 8

[11]. Epstein, Mark. Thoughts Without a Thinker. New York, NY. Basicbooks, A Division of Harper Collins Publishers, Inc., 1995. p. 128

[12]. Shapiro, Deb. Your Body Speaks your Mind. Boulder, Colorado. Sounds True, Inc., 2006. *i-xxi*

BIBLIOGRAPHY

American Psychiatric Association. Diagnostic and Statistical Manual of Mental Disorders. New York, New York. American Psychiatric Publishing, 5 Edition, 2013.

Bolte Taylor, Jill. My Stroke of Insight: A Brain Scientist's Personal Journey. New York, New York. Viking, 2008.

Breggin, Peter R. Talking Back to Prozac: What Doctors Aren't Telling you About Today's Most Controversial Drug. New York, New York. St. Martin's Press,1994.

Chodron, Pema. When Things Fall Apart. Boston, Massachusetts. Shambala Publications,1997.

Chodron, Pema. This Moment is the Perfect Teacher. Shambala Audio, 2008.

Dalai Lama. The Joy of Living and Dying in Peace: Core Teachings of Tibetan Buddhism. San Francisco, CA. HarperSanFrancisco, 1997.

Dalai Lama. The Tibetan Book of the Dead: The Great Book of Natural Liberation Through Understanding in the Between. New York, New York. Penguin Group, 2006.

Dayton, Tian. Heartwounds: The Impact of Unresolved Trauma on Relationships. Deerfield Beach, Florida. Health Communications, Inc., 1997.

Epstein, Mark. Going to Pieces Without Falling Apart. New York, NY. Broadway Books, 1998.

Epstein, Mark. Thoughts Without a Thinker. New York, NY. Basicbooks, A Division of Harper Collins Publishers, Inc., 1995.

Frederickson, Barbra. Positivity: Groundbreaking Research Reveals How to Embrace The Hidden Strengths of Positive

Emotions, Overcome Negativity, and Thrive. New York, New York. Crown Archetype, 2009.

Halifax, Joan. The Fruitful Darkness. New York, New York. Grove Press, 1993.

Hillman, James. Suicide and the Soul. New York, New York. Harper and Row, 1998.

James, John and Friedman, Russell. The Grief Recovery Handbook. New York, New York. Harper Collins, 1998.

Joiner, Thomas. Myths About Suicide. Cambridge, Massachusetts. Harvard University Press, 2011.

Lewis, C.S. A Grief Observed. London, England, Faber, 1961.

Lukas, Christopher and Seiden, Henry. Silent Grief: Living in the Wake of Suicide. New York, New York. Charles Scribner's Sons, 1987.

Noel, Brook. I Wasn't Ready to Say Goodbye: Surviving, Coping, and Healing After the Sudden Death of a Loved One. Milwaukee, Wisconsin. Champion Press, Ltd, 2000.

Pope, Kenneth S., Ph.D., ABPP & Vasquez, Melba, J.T., Ph.D, ABPP. Ethics in Psychotherapy and Counseling: A Practical Guide, 3rd Edition. San Francisco, California. Jossey-Bass, an imprint of John Wiley, Publishers, 2007.

Shapiro, Deb. Your Body Speaks your Mind. Boulder, Colorado. Sounds True, Inc., 2006.

Styron, William. Darkness Visible: A Memoir of Madness. New York, New York. Random House, 1990.

Toffler, Alvin. Future Shock. New York, New York. Random House, 1970.

Tolle, Eckhart. A New Earth: Awakening to Your Life's Purpose. New York. Dutton, A member of Penguin Group (USA), Inc., 2005.

Tolle, Eckhart. The Power of Now: A Guide to Spiritual Enlightenment. Novato, California. New World Library, 1999.

WEBSITES

Dsm5.org.
http://www.dsm5.org/PROPOSEDREVISION/Pages/TraumaandStressorRelatedDisorders.aspx

Suicidology.org

Survivorsofsuicide

Made in United States
North Haven, CT
07 October 2022

25128676R00125